introducti

Welcome to Edinburgh – The Capital Guide.
For those of you who have seen the Guide in the past, you will notice many, many changes for this latest edition.

The first is visual: apart from the new design and layout we've changed the format from the rather boring A5 size to this quite unusual square book. We have done this because it's completely different and gives us much more room to expand the content – which we have done. However, it is still easy to carry around with you.

Inside you will find a much more comprehensive and objective (DEFINITELY not advertising driven) guide to the huge number of pubs, clubs and restaurants that Edinburgh has to offer, as well as the many sights there are to see and visit. We have also extended our coverage of 'retail therapy' not for the sake of it, but because there is so much that our city has to offer in this area.

The descriptions are written in a "chatty" style to allow us more freedom to convey to you the ambiance and style of these locations. There are many guides that will give you a purely factual or advertorial view of the city; what we have tried to do is give you the equivalent of a good friend who knows the city and who is more than happy to show you around while you're here. We will undoubtedly have missed out or forgotten a few places that should or would be included and we ran out of room for some of those we wanted to mention, so please don't assume that if something isn't in, it's not worth visiting. We simply hope that with over ... ants and shops and just under that number of pubs to choose from, you'll get enough of a flavour of the city to find whatever you're looking for, whatever your tastes are.

For your guidance we have split Edinburgh into 6 areas covering: The Old Town and Bridges; The New Town and Stockbridge; The East End and Portobello; The West End and Lothian Road; The South Side, Tollcross and Morningside; and Leith. Each area has its own map to help you find your way around and on these maps we have located where the advertisers can be found.

All these changes have been made in our quest to produce the best guide of its kind around and this year we believe we have succeeded. Clearly, because of its minimal cover price, we have to rely on advertising to fund the publication.

For £2.00 you have just bought yourself the best Guide to take you around our Capital City. The editorial is atmospheric without losing its purpose, and the advertising is integrated in a way that enhances the usefulness of our Guide.

One thing that hasn't changed is that we are continuing to offer a bottle of malt whisky to the best critical, but constructive, letter we receive during the course of the next year.

So, we hope you enjoy the read and we look forward to hearing from you. Enjoy your stay in Edinburgh.

This edition published by **Pastime Publications Ltd**, 5/9 Rennie's Isle, Edinburgh EH6 6QA.
Tel/Fax: 0131 553 4444
E-mail: pastime@btconnect.com

Written and edited by Justin Anderson

2002 © Pastime Publications Ltd. No part of Edinburgh: The Capital Guide 2002/2003 may be published or reproduced in any form without the prior consent of the publisher

Photography by Steve Godfrey

Pastime Publications are proud to have been accepted as members of Scotland the Brand, an organisation committed to promoting the excellence of Scottish products, services and facilities throughout Scotland and the World. The distinctive blue and red tartan Scotland mark signifies outstanding quality.

Printed and bound in Scotland
UK and Worldwide distribution

VISIT THE PALACE THAT CALLED ITSELF A YACHT

The Royal Yacht *Britannia* has moved to her final berth at Ocean Terminal, Edinburgh's stylish new waterfront retail and leisure development in the historic port of Leith.

Discover her fascinating story on a tour that begins in the new Visitor Centre which is now located on the second floor of Ocean Terminal. Then with an audio handset, tour five decks on board. Highlights include artefacts from The Royal Collection, the magnificent State Dining and Drawing Rooms and the gleaming Engine Room.

There is now even more to see with the opening of more areas including the Royal Marines Barracks, the Laundry and the Sick Bay.

Britannia is located only 2 miles from the city centre. If you are arriving by car there is parking within Ocean Terminal, alternatively Lothian Buses run frequent services from the city centre (no.22) and Guide Friday and MacTours run buses from Waverley Bridge.

THE ROYAL YACHT
BRITANNIA

welcome

to Edinburgh, what would you like to do...?

Edinburgh's history

To give you a flavour of the events which have shaped the city known as the *Athens of the North* and *Auld Reekie*, we've put together a timeline with many of the events that have made it what it is today.

Pre-Roman Castle Rock first known to be inhabited and was the site of many Celtic feasts.

Early 7th Century Kingdom of Gododdin (known by the Romans as Votadini) is centred on Castle Rock, ruled by King Mynydogg. His capital, Dun Eidyn (the fortress on the hill slope) is on the rock itself.

626 Edwin of Northumbria takes the town and renames it Edinburgh, an anglification of Dun Eidyn.

1018 Malcolm II defeats the Northumbrians and confirms Edinburgh as a Scottish town.

1040 MacBeth kills Duncan to become King of Scotland.

1057 Malcolm Canmore kills MacBeth. Macbeth's stepson, Lulach, known as 'The Fool', briefly takes the throne.

1058 Malcolm Canmore kills Lulach and is crowned King Malcolm III.

1093 After the death of Queen Margaret, wife of Malcolm III, Edinburgh Castle first appears in recorded history.

1124 David I, son of Malcolm III and Margaret, is crowned.

1128 Holyrood Abbey is founded by David I, after an escape from a mighty stag while out hunting in the area.

1249 Queen Margaret is canonised and becomes St Margaret. (St Margaret's chapel is the oldest remaining part of Edinburgh Castle)

1286 Alexander III dies leaving only his infant granddaughter, the *Maid of Norway*, as heir to the throne of Scotland.

1290 Margaret, the Maid of Norway, dies leaving no clear heir to the throne and thirteen claimants. Edward I of England is invited to settle the dispute by the Scots in an attempt to avoid civil war. Edward subsequently claims lordship over Scotland

1292 After a long dispute between two descendants of David I, Balliol and Bruce, John Balliol is appointed King under the feudal lordship of Edward I.

1295 John Balliol revolts against Edward I and establishes the Auld Alliance with France, whereby both countries agree to invade England should England attack either of them.

1296 Edinburgh Castle is sacked by Edward I. John Balliol surrenders and is taken to England and imprisoned.

1297 William Wallace leads Scots to a great victory over the English at Stirling Bridge. Wallace is knighted and appointed Guardian of the Realm, acting for John Balliol.

1298 Wallace's forces are wiped out by Edward I's army at Falkirk. Edward effectively re-establishes his feudality over Scotland.

1305 Wallace is captured and tried for treason in London, found guilty and hanged, drawn and quartered.

1306 Robert the Bruce kills John Comyn, a rival for the throne, in Greyfriar's Church, Dumfries. He then goes to Scone where he is crowned King of Scotland.

1307 Robert the Bruce defeats the newly crowned Edward II at the Battle of Louden Hill.

1313 An assault party scales the north face of Castle Rock and seizes Edinburgh Castle back from the English for Robert the Bruce.

1314 Robert the Bruce wins a famous victory over the English at Bannockburn and takes full control of Scotland back from Edward II.

1320 Against Edward II's attempts to take back control of Scotland, the Declaration of Arbroath is issued to the Pope, including the famous lines: *"It is not for honour nor riches, nor glory that we fight but for liberty alone, which no true man lays down except with his life."* and *"…as long as but a hundred of us remain alive, never will we on any conditions be brought under English rule."*

1322 Holyrood Abbey is sacked by the English.

1328 Treaty of Edinburgh-Northampton ends war with English and concedes Scotland's independence.

1329 Robert the Bruce dies and his heart is taken from his body and preserved. David II is crowned King.

1368 Rebuilding begins on the ruined Castle.

1371 Robert II, the first of the royal Stewart line, is crowned after the death of David II without producing an heir.

1390 Robert III takes the throne after his father's abdication.

1400 Henry IV unsuccessfully lays siege to Edinburgh Castle.

1406 James, the only surviving son of Robert III, is captured by pirates en route to France and handed over to Henry IV as a prisoner. Robert dies within days of receiving the news and the Duke of Albany is appointed Regent during James' incarceration.

1424 After the death of Albany and the promotion of his incompetent son Murdoch to the Regency, the Scots secure James' release from Henry V with the Treaty of London, subject to a £40,000 ransom. James is crowned James I at Scone. Murdoch is beheaded along with his two sons and the Earl of Lennox for failing to secure James' release sooner.

1437 James I is murdered in Perth by a group of conspirators led by Sir Robert Graham, under the orders of his grandfather the Earl of Atholl. Graham and Atholl are both executed. James II is crowned at the age of six.

1450 The Scots defeat the English at the Battle of Sark. James II grants permission for a wall to be built around Edinburgh to protect against further invasion by the English. The north pastures are flooded to form the Nor Loch.

1460 James II is killed during a siege of Roxburgh Castle. James III comes to the throne and formally acknowledges Edinburgh as the capital of Scotland. He turns Edinburgh Castle into an ordnance factory.

1488 A group of nobles led by Prince James rise against James III and defeat him in battle at Sauchieburn. James III is found dead a few days later. James is crowned James IV.

1498 The Palace of Holyroodhouse is founded.

1513 James IV and many other Scots die at Flodden in a disastrous battle with the English. The Flodden Wall is built around Edinburgh as a further defence against the English, taking in the Cowgate. The wall is 23 feet tall and 5 feet deep. The heir to the throne, James V, is only 17 months old when his father dies.

1524 James V is crowned in Holyrood Abbey.

1542 James V dies after defeat by Henry VIII's forces at the Battle of Solway Moss. His infant daughter Mary Stewart becomes Mary Queen of Scots. Several Regents are appointed during her minority.

1543 The Treaty of Greenwich ends the war with England, but one provision of the deal is that Mary Queen of Scots will be married to Prince Edward, Henry's heir.

Royal Museum
Museum of Scotland

Presenting Scotland to the World and the World to Scotland

These two 'must-see' Museums stand side-by-side in the centre of the city, minutes from the historic Royal Mile and Edinburgh Castle.

Royal Museum
Explore this elegant Victorian building, distinguished by its soaring glass-topped roof and stunning Main Hall. Here you will discover outstanding international collections of Decorative Arts, Science and Industry, Archaeology and the Natural World. Daily Guided Tours: Special Events: Roof Terrace: exhibIT electronic resource room: Discovery Centre: Soupson soup bar: Cafe Delos: Shop

Museum of Scotland
A striking new landmark in Edinburgh's historic Old Town. This Museum presents for the first time the history of Scotland - its land, its people and their achievements - through the rich national collections. The stunning series of galleries take you from Scotland's geological beginnings through time to the twentieth century.

Royal Museum & Museum of Scotland
Chambers Street
Edinburgh
EH1 1JF

Opening hours
Monday to Saturday 10am - 5pm
Tuesday 10am - 8pm
Sunday 12 noon - 5pm

Telephone 0131 247 4219 (Royal Museum)
Telephone 0131 247 4422 (Museum of Scotland)
Textphone 0131 247 4027
Fax 0131 220 4819

www.nms.ac.uk
Admission Free

Scottish
TOURIST BOARD
★★★★★
MUSEUM

1544 Infuriated by the Scots' reneging on the agreement to marry the infant Mary Queen of Scots to Prince Edward, in order to keep Scotland neutral when he invades France, Henry VIII orders the Earl of Hertford to *"Sack Leith and burn and subvert it and all the rest, putting man, woman and child to fire and sword without exception."* This he does – Leith and Edinburgh, as well as several Borders towns, are sacked and burned, with the entire Old Town and Castle destroyed, excepting St Margaret's Chapel, which still stands today. This becomes known as the "Rough Wooing".

1554 Mary of Guise, widow of James V and mother to Mary Queen of Scots, becomes sole Regent for her daughter.

1558 Mary Queen of Scots is married to Francis II, Dauphin of France.

1559 Henry II of France dies, leaving Francis II as King of France and Scotland, by virtue of his marriage to Mary Queen of Scots. In June of the year, Mary of Guise dies of "dropsy". By the end of the year, Francis II is dead of a septic ear and Mary makes plans to return to Scotland. John Knox, a Calvinist and Protestant Reformer, becomes Minister of the High Kirk of Edinburgh at St Giles.

1560 The French abandon all claims to Scotland in the Treaty of Edinburgh. Parliament introduces the Protestant Order and makes Scotland legally Protestant.

1561 Mary returns to Scotland to take control of the country.

1565 Mary Queen of Scots marries Henry, Lord Darnley in Holyrood Abbey.

1566 James VI is born in Edinburgh Castle to Mary Queen of Scots and Darnley. Later, her confidant and secretary, Rizzio, is murdered at Holyroodhouse.

1567 Darnley is murdered in suspicious circumstances. Mary marries her lover, the Earl of Bothwell. Mary is later imprisoned in Edinburgh. After being moved to Loch Leven, she is forced to abdicate in favour of her son James VI.

1568 Mary escapes incarceration and raises a small army, but she is defeated at the battle of Langside. She flees to England, where Elizabeth I places her under house arrest, where she remains for 19 years.

1583 Edinburgh University is founded.

1587 Mary Queen of Scots is executed at Fotheringay Castle by order of Elizabeth I.

1597 James VI publishes his book about witchcraft, *Daemonologie.*

1603 After the death of Queen Elizabeth, James VI takes the English throne and unites the crowns, becoming James VI and I.

1625 Charles I is crowned in Holyrood Abbey after the death of his father James VI.

1645 Plague wipes out Edinburgh's population, leading to many closes, including Mary King's Close, being sealed up with the dying still inside. Of 40,000 citizens, 60 are declared fit to bear arms and defend the town.

1649 Charles I is executed. Scots appoint Charles II king under the condition that he agrees to their religious policies.

1650 Edinburgh is taken by Oliver Cromwell. Under his protectorate, a royalist supporter of Charles II, the Marquis of Montrose, is paraded through Edinburgh by the Earl of Argyll, before being hanged, beheaded and quartered. His head is hung on the Tolbooth.

1660 Charles II is restored to the throne. The Earl of Argyll suffers the same fate as Montrose before him, being beheaded and having his head placed atop the Tolbooth.

1671 A reconstruction of Holyroodhouse is ordered to repair the damage caused by Hertford and Cromwell.

1685 Charles II dies in England. His brother James VII and II takes the throne.

1688 Roman Catholic King James VII and II is deposed by Parliament and rule is handed over to the Protestant Queen Mary II and her Husband, William of Orange, a Dutch prince, who becomes William II of Scotland and III of England.

1689 Roman Catholic the Duke of Gordon loses Edinburgh Castle to the Protestant forces of William of Orange. Jacobite forces supporting the deposed James VII are defeated at the battle of Killiecrankie.

1692 The Campbells, having sworn loyalty to Queen Mary and William of Orange, slaughter the MacDonalds at Glencoe, for missing the set deadline to swear their own oath.

1694 Mary II dies leaving the throne in the sole hands of William of Orange.

1695 The Bank of Scotland is established by an Act of Parliament.

1702 William and is succeeded by his daughter Anne as Queen of England and Scotland.

1707 The Treaty of Union is signed in Edinburgh, handing political control of Scotland over to England. The Edinburgh Mob riots in protest.

1711 David Hume, famous philosopher and historian, is born in Edinburgh.

1714 George I, great grandson of James VI and I, takes the throne after the death of Anne, marking the beginning of the Georgian era.

CELEBRATING
70 YEARS

The National Trust
for Scotland

For a great day out in Edinburgh

GLADSTONE'S LAND

Royal Mile

This atmospheric merchant's house reflects life in Edinburgh's Old Town 300 years ago. Cloth was traded from here and the accommodation is typical of the era. Replicas of 17th-century goods, fine furnishings and paintings. Children's guidebook. Shop.
OPEN 1 April-31 October: Mon-Sat 10-5; Sun 2-5
Entry £3.50 (£2.50)

GEORGIAN HOUSE

7 Charlotte Square

Two hundred years ago, this was a fashionable society house. Learn about New Town life from the beautiful furnishings, paintings and household items. Children's guidebook. Shop.
OPEN 1 March-24 December
    (Mar-Oct: Mon-Fri 10-5; Sun 2-5)
     (Nov-Dec: Mon-Sat 11-4; Sun 2-4)
      Entry £5 (£4)

Nos 27 & 28 CHARLOTTE SQUARE

These fine Robert Adam buildings now house a display of 20th-century Scottish paintings. Fine furnishings create the ambience of an 1820s Drawing Room. Below the gallery is a Coffee House and Shop, while in the evening the five-star 'Taste of Scotland' Restaurant at No 27 offers a wide selection of Scottish dishes.
OPEN All Year
Gallery: Mon-Sat 10-5; Sun 12-5
(last admission 4.45)
Shop: Mon-Sat 10-5.30; Sun 10-5
Coffee House: daily 10-6
Restaurant: daily 6pm-11pm
Free entry

1723 Adam Smith, famous political economist, is born in Edinburgh.

1727 George II takes the throne after his father's death.

1736 The Edinburgh Mob riots and hangs disgraced City Guard Captain John Porteous in the Grassmarket.

1744 The Honourable Company of Edinburgh Golfers becomes the first official golf club in recorded history.

1745 Prince Charles Edward Stuart (Bonnie Prince Charlie), grandson of James VII, briefly occupies the city with his Jacobite supporters and demands the surrender of the Castle. The Castle withstands and barrages the Prince.

1746 Bonnie Prince Charlie's Jacobite forces are eventually crushed at Culloden, after a foray into England.

1760 George III is crowned.

1765 A section of the Nor Loch is drained as work begins on the North Bridge. The rest of the Loch is eventually drained to form Princes Street Gardens.

1767 Building begins on the New Town designed by James Craig.

1771 Sir Walter Scott, famous novelist, is born in Edinburgh.

1772 After the first effort had collapsed, the redeveloped North Bridge is opened.

1780 The beginnings of The Mound are seen, as tailor George Boyd makes a track of stones and planks to traverse the swamp that the Nor Loch had left behind. After much dumping of rubbish from the building of the New Town, The Mound is eventually formed some years later.

1785 The first foundation stone is laid for South Bridge.

1786 South Bridge is opened to foot traffic.

1787 Deacon Brodie begins his dual career as a burglar.

1788 Brodie is arrested in Holland, trying to flee to America. He is brought back to Edinburgh and hanged. Building on the South Bridge is completed.

1816 The Nelson Monument is built on Calton Hill to commemorate Nelson's victory in the Battle of Trafalgar.

1820 George IV is crowned.

1822 George IV makes a famous visit to Edinburgh, holding court in Holyroodhouse and adopting Highland dress. Building begins on Playfair's National Monument on Calton Hill, to commemorate those who died in the Napoleonic wars. It is planned to be a full replica of the Parthenon, but funds run out and only a fragment is actually built.

1824 The Great Fire of Edinburgh burns the top half of the Royal Mile, even collapsing the wooden spire atop the Tron Kirk.

1826 William Burke meets William Hare in Edinburgh.

1827 Work begins on George IV Bridge.

1828 Burke and Hare commit their infamous murders.

1829 William Burke is hanged for multiple murders. Hare is set free for turning state's evidence against his partner. William III and IV is crowned.

1830 Edinburgh's population has doubled from just 30 years ago as the Highland Clearances, the Irish Famine and mass unemployment in the countryside caused by the Industrial Revolution attract thousands of immigrants to the city.

1836 George IV Bridge is opened.

1837 Queen Victoria takes the throne.

1840 The New Town is completed.

1846 The Scott Monument is completed in memory of Sir Walter Scott. Edinburgh is joined by rail to London for the first time.

1850 Robert Louis Stevenson, famous author and creator of *Jekyll and Hyde*, is born in Edinburgh.

1853 Camera Obscura is established by Maria Theresa Short, an optician.

1890 The Forth Rail Bridge is opened.

1901 Edward I and III is crowned

1910 George V is crowned

1927 The Prince of Wales opens the Scottish National War Memorial at the Castle.

1936 Edward II and IV is crowned, but abdicates the throne in order to marry Mrs Simpson, an American divorcee. His brother George VI takes the throne instead.

1947 The first Edinburgh Festival takes place

1952 After the death of her father George VI, Queen Elizabeth I and II is crowned.

1964 The Forth Road Bridge is opened.

1966 Heriot Watt University is founded.

1997 Scotland votes for a devolved Parliament.

1999 Presiding Officer David Steel opens the new Scottish Parliament with the words: *"The Scottish Parliament, adjourned on 25th March 1707, is hereby reconvened."*

2002 Elizabeth I and II celebrates her Golden Jubilee year.

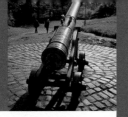

sight-seeing

OLD TOWN AND BRIDGES

BRASS RUBBING CENTRE
Trinity Apse, Chalmers Close, Royal Mile.
Weekdays 10.00-17.00; Suns during Festival 2.00-17.00. Free.
Tel: 0131 556 4364.

A charge is made for every rubbing, which includes cost of materials and a royalty to the churches where applicable.

CAMERA OBSCURA
Castlehill, top of Royal Mile, next to Edinburgh Castle.
Apr-Oct, daily 09.30-18.00 (later in Jul & Aug). Nov-Mar daily 10.00-17.00. Entrance charge.
Gift shop. Tel: 0131 226 3709.

High in the unusual Outlook Tower an 1800's "cinema" shows live images of Edinburgh.

CANONGATE KIRK
Canongate, Royal Mile.

The church, built by order of James VII in 1688, is the Parish Church of the Canongate and also the Kirk of Holyroodhouse and Edinburgh Castle.

CITY ART CENTRE
Market Street
Open Jun-Sep, Mon-Sat, 10.00-18.00, Sun during Festival, 14.00-17.00. Oct-May Mon-Sat 10.00-17.00, usually free, occasionally charges for special exhibitions.
Tel: 0131 200 2000

The City of Edinburgh's Art Gallery. A converted warehouse on four floors with a programme of changing exhibitions and displays from the City's collection of paintings.

EDINBURGH CASTLE
Castle Rock, top of the Royal Mile.
Apr-Sept; daily 09.30-18.00 (last entry). Oct-March daily 09.30-17.00 (last entry). Castle closes 45 mins after last entry. Entrance charge. Parking available. (HS).
Tel: 0131 244 3101.

One of the most famous castles in the world, whose battlements overlook the Esplanade where the floodlit Military Tattoo is staged each year late August to early September. The Castle stands on a rock which has been a fortress from time immemorial.

GLADSTONE'S LAND
(The NTS) 477B Lawnmarket; Royal Mile.
1 Apr-31 Oct; Mon-Sat 10.00-17.00. Sun 14.00-17.00. (last admission 16.00pm)
Entrance Charge.
Tel: 0131 226 5856.

Gladstone's Land was the home of a prosperous Edinburgh merchant in the seventeenth century. On the Royal Mile, near the castle, it is decorated and furnished with great authenticity to give visitors an impression of life in Edinburgh's Old Town some 300 years ago.

GREYFRIAR'S BOBBY
Corner of George IV Bridge and Candlemaker Row.
All times. Free.

Statue of Greyfriar's Bobby the Skye terrier who, after his master's death in 1858, watched over his grave in the nearby Greyfriar's Kirkyard for 14 years.

GREYFRIAR'S KIRK
Greyfriar's Place, south end of George IV Bridge.
Easter-End Oct Mon-Fri 10.30-16.30, Sat 10.30-14.30. Kirkyard 09.00-18.00 Free. Gift/bookshop, museum, video
Tel: 0131 225 1900.

The Kirk, dedicated on Christmas Day 1620, was the scene of the adoption and signing of the National Covenant - a copy is on display. The kirkyard, inaugurated in 1562, on the site of a 15th century Franciscan Friary, contains fine Scottish monuments of 17th century: (in 1679, more than 1000 Covenanters were imprisoned there). The Martyrs Monument and memorials to Greyfriars Bobby and his master John Grey can be seen there.

HUNTLY HOUSE
Canongate, Royal Mile.
Jun-Sep, Mon-Sat 10.00-17.00; Sun during Festival 14.00-17.00. Free.
Tel: 0131 200 2000.

Built in 1570, this fine house was later associated with members of the Huntly Family. It is now a city museum illustrating Edinburgh life down the ages and contains important collections of Edinburgh silver and glass and Scottish pottery.

Whisky galore and a whole lot more

- Scotch Whisky Tour including a free taste of whisky for adults. Meet our resident ghost and take a barrel ride through Scotch whisky history.

- Whisky Bar with over 270 different whiskies.

- 'Taste of Scotland' Restaurant and Coffee Shop.

- Gift shop with extensive range of whisky including rare and unusual brands.

The Scotch Whisky Heritage Centre, 354 Castehill (beside Edinburgh Castle), The Royal Mile, Edinburgh EH1 2NE. Tel: 0131 220 0441 Fax: 0131 220 6288 Email: enquiry@whisky-heritage.co.uk Web: www.whisky-heritage.co.uk

INVESTOR IN PEOPLE

Scottish THISTLE AWARDS 1998 WINNER

Experience the return of the Ice Age to Edinburrrrrgh.

Enjoy the most fantastic journey on Earth. Travel back in time and witness the Big Bang. Be shaken by earthquakes and face boiling lava, fly over glaciers and dive deep beneath the oceans. You could even get caught in a tropical rainstorm. Visit Our Dynamic Earth and you'll have the experience of a lifetime.

Our Dynamic Earth Holyrood Road Edinburgh EH8 8AS **T** 0131 550 7800
web www.dynamicearth.co.uk

JOHN KNOX HOUSE

43 High Street, Royal Mile.
All year - Mon-Sat 10.00-16.30. Entrance charge
Tel: 0131 556 9579/2647.

A picturesque 15th century house connected with John Knox, the famous Scottish reformer.

LADY STAIRS HOUSE

Off Lawnmarket, Royal Mile.
Jun-Sept, Mon-Sat 10.00-18.00; Oct-May, Mon-Sat 10.00-17.00;
Sun during Festival 14.00-17.00. Free. Gift shop.
Tel: 0131 200 2000.

Built in 1622, this now houses The Writer's Museum, dedicated to Scotland's great literary figures, most notably Burns, Scott and Stevenson.

MUSEUM OF CHILDHOOD

42 High Street, Royal Mile
Mon-Sat 10.00-17.00, Sun during Festival 14.00-17.00. Free.
Tel: 0131 529 4142.

This unique museum has a fine collection of toys, dolls, dolls' houses, costumes and nursery equipment.

MUSEUM OF FIRE

Lauriston Place.
Visitors by arrangement with Fire Brigade Headquarters. Free.
(Lothians & Borders Fire Brigade). No parking.
Tel: 0131 228 2401.

Guided tours round the museum, with its collection of old uniforms, equipment and engines, subject to the availability of a Fireman Guide.

PALACE OF HOLYROODHOUSE

Foot of the Royal Mile.
Nov-Mar 09.30-16.30; (last admission 15.45). Apr- Oct 09.30-18.00 (last admission 17.15). The Palace is also closed during Royal and State Visits and for periods before and after visits; check dates.
Tel: 0131 556 7371/1096 (recorded information).

Official residence of the Queen in Scotland. Founded in 1498, it was restored to its current state in 1671 after repairs were required to the damage done by Hertford in 1544 and that done by a fire accidentally caused by Cromwell's troops when they took the city.

PARLIAMENT HOUSE

Parliament Square, behind the High Kirk of St. Giles, Royal Mile.
All year, Mon-Fri 09.00-17.00. Free. Tel: 0131 225 2595.

Built 1632-39 this was the seat of Scottish government until 1707, when the governments of Scotland and England were united. Now the Supreme Law Courts of Scotland

THE PEOPLE'S STORY

Canongate Tolbooth, Royal Mile.
Mon-Sat 10.00-17.00 (June to Sept 10.00-18.00). During the Edinburgh Festival: Sun 14.00-17.00. Free. Tel: 0131 200 2000.

The Canongate Tolbooth, which was built in 1591, now houses The People's Story. The museum tells of the lives, works and leisure of ordinary people in the Scottish capital from the late 18th century to the present day.

ROYAL MUSEUM AND MUSEUM OF SCOTLAND

Chambers Street.
Jan-Dec, Mon-Sat 10.00-17.00. Tues 10.00-20.00. Sun 12.00-17.00. Admission free Tearoom. Disabled access. Tel: 0131 247 4027.

Part of the National Museums of Scotland, the Royal Museum is set in a fine Victorian building while the Museum of Scotland sits nearby in a striking new, architecturally acclaimed home. The Royal houses the national collections of decorative arts of the world, ethnography, natural history, geology, technology and science. The Museum of Scotland presents Scotland's history from geological beginnings through our rich national connections.

ST. CECILIA'S HALL

Cowgate, at the foot of Niddry Street.
Jan-Dec. Wed, Sat 14.00-17.00. During Festival, Mon-Sat 10.30-12.30. Entrance charge. Gift shop. Tel: 0131 650 2805.

Scotland's oldest concert hall, built to a design by Robert Milne in 1762, for the Edinburgh Musical Society.

ST. GILES' CATHEDRAL

High Street; Royal Mile.
Winter: Mon-Sat 09.00-17.00. Sun 12.00-17.00. Summer: Mon-Sat 09.00-19.00, Sun 13.00-17.00. Also open for services. Occasionally closed for weddings, ceremonies, etc. Please check before travelling any distance. Free (donation for Thistle Chapel). Restaurant serving home-made food and shop selling souvenirs of St. Giles' and Scotland. Tel: 0131 225 9442.

There has been a church here since the 9th century. Of the present building, the tower is late 15th century. At one time it was divided between four congregations and also included space for a weaver's workshop and storage for the burgh's guillotine – known as 'The Maiden'. See also the exquisite Thistle Chapel. In the street outside the west door is the Heart of Midlothian, a heart shaped design in the cobblestones. It marks the site of the Old Tolbooth, built in 1466, which was stormed in the 1736 Porteous Riots and demolished in 1817.

SCOTCH WHISKY HERITAGE CENTRE

354 Castlehill, The Royal Mile, Edinburgh EH1 2NE.

Open all year Summer 10.00-17.30. Extended hours in summer (Only closed 25/12 & 1/1) Concession and group rates available.
Tel: 0131 220 0441

The award winning Scotch Whisky Heritage Centre, located beside Edinburgh Castle, gives the equivalent of a distillery tour in the heart of Edinburgh's Old Town. Visitors learn how and where Scotch whiskies are made with a tour and A.V. shows. A ghostly presentation of the art of the master blender precedes a journey through time on a whisky barrel (with commentary in a choice of 8 languages). There is a free taste of whisky for adults before viewing the centre's whisky and gift shop (also open Sundays).

TALBOT RICE GALLERY

University of Edinburgh, Old College, South Bridge.

Tues-Sat 10.00-17.00. Usually free.
Tel: 0131 650 2210/1/2/3.

Edinburgh University's Torrie Collection and changing exhibitions are on public display in this fine building.

SIR JULES THORNE HISTORICAL MUSEUM

At rear of Royal College of Surgeons of Edinburgh, 18 Nicolson Street.

Jan-Dec exc. public holidays. Mon-Fri 14.00-16.00.
Free. Donations invited.
Tel: 0131 527 1600.

Historic exhibition of 'Edinburgh and Medicine'. Lower floor of the hall illustrates the history of surgery in general, and Edinburgh's special contribution from 1505 to the present.

UNIVERSITY COLLECTION OF HISTORIC MUSICAL INSTRUMENTS

Reid Concert Hall, Bristo Square.

All year, Wed 15.00-17.00, Sat 10.00-13.00. Free.
Tel: 0131 447 4791 & 0131 650 2423.

The collection now consists of over 1,000 instruments and is maintained by the University for the purposes of research, performance and support for teaching.

WHITEHORSE CLOSE

Off Canongate, Royal Mile.

A restored group of 17th-century buildings off the High Street. The coaches to London left from White Horse Inn (named after Queen Mary's Palfrey), and there are Jacobite links.

NEW TOWN and STOCKBRIDGE

GENERAL REGISTER HOUSE

East end of Princes Street.

Jan-Dec. Legal: 09.30-16.30. Historical: 09.00-16.45 (last admission 16.25). Exhibitions: 10.00-16.00. Free.
Tel: 0131 535 1314.

This fine Robert Adam building, founded 1774, is the headquarters of the Scottish Record Office and the home of the national archive of Scotland.

NATIONAL GALLERY OF SCOTLAND

The Mound.

Mon-Sat 10.00-1700 (extended hours during Festival). Sun 12.00-17.00. Free.
Tel: 0131 624 6200. www.natgalscot.ac.uk

One of the most distinguished of the smaller galleries of Europe, the National Gallery of Scotland contains a comprehensive collection of old masters, impressionist and Scottish paintings. This includes masterpieces by Raphael, El Greco, Rembrandt, Constable, Titian, Velasquez, Raeburn, Van Gogh and Gaugin. Currently undergoing a major renovation under "The Playfair Project" named after the original architect, William Playfair.

ROYAL BOTANIC GARDEN

Entrance off Inverleith Row and Arboretum Place.

Open daily (except Dec 25 and Jan 1) from 9.30am. Admission free, voluntary donations scheme at The Glasshouse Experience. Guided tours (April-September) Terrace Cafe and Botanics Shop with delightful gifts and plants.
Tel: 0131 552 7171.

Scotland's National Botanic Garden displays plant treasures from around the globe in its seventy exquisitely landscaped acres. The Garden boasts a world-famous Rock Garden and ten magnificent glasshouses including Britain's tallest Palm House, with plants from the temperate and tropical parts of the world. Just 1 mile from the City Centre, this beautiful oasis has spectacular views of the Edinburgh skyline as well as events, exhibitions and activities all year round.

ROYAL SCOTTISH ACADEMY

At foot of Mound, on Princes Street.

Mon-Sat 10.00-17.00, Sun 14.00-17.00. Entrance charge.
Tel: 0131 225 6671.

The Academy has annual exhibitions and special Festival exhibitions. Ramped wheelchair entrance at back.

SCOTT MONUMENT
In Princes Street Gardens.

Completed in 1844, a statue of Sir Walter Scott and his dog Maida, under a canopy and spire 200 feet high, with 64 statuettes of Scott characters.

SCOTTISH NATIONAL PORTRAIT GALLERY
East end of Queen Street

Mon-Sat 10.00-17.00 (extended hours during Festival), Sun 12.00-17.00. Free. Print Room and Reference Section open 10.00-12.00, 14.30-16.30 Mon-Fri. Cafe.
Tel: 0131 624 6200. www.natgalscot.ac.uk

Illustrates the history of Scotland through portraits of the famous men and women who contributed to it in all fields of activity from the 16th century to the present day such as Mary, Queen of Scots, James VI and I, Flora MacDonald, Robert Burns, Sir Walter Scott, David Hume and Ramsay MacDonald.

WEST END and LOTHIAN ROAD

DEAN GALLERY
Belford Road.

All year - Mon-Sat 10.00-17.00, Sun 12.00-17.00. Free. Parking available. Cafe.
Tel: 0131 624 6200. www.natgalscot.ac.uk

Extensive collection of Dada and Surrealist art. Also modern and contemporary art exhibitions.

DEAN VILLAGE
Bell's Brae, off Queensferry Street on Water of Leith.

There was grain milling in this notable village of Edinburgh for over 800 years. The view downstream through the high arches of Dean Bridge is among the most picturesque in the city.

GEORGIAN HOUSE
(The NTS), No.7 Charlotte Square.

Apr-Oct Mon-Sat 10.00-17.00. Sun 14.00-17.00. (last admission 4.30pm). Entrance charge.
Tel: 0131 225 2160.

The north side of Charlotte Square is Robert Adam's masterpiece of urban architecture – a splendid example of the neo-classical 'palace front'. The three floors of No.7, The Georgian House, are delightfully furnished as they would have been around 1796. Adjacent to the shop is an audio visual room where video programmes describe the history of Edinburgh's New Town and in more dramatic form 'A Day in the life of The Georgian House'.

GORGIE CITY FARM PROJECT
51 Gorgie Road.

Mar-Oct (Daily) 9.30-16.30. Nov-Feb (Daily) 9.30-16.00, exc. Xmas and New Years Day. Free. Car and mini-bus parking only. Tearoom.
Tel: 0131 337 4202.

A variety of animals, pens and a farm kitchen with workshop/craft facilities.

ST. CUTHBERTS CHURCH
Lothian Road.

Open with guides Jun-Sep, Mon-Fri 10.30-15.30; other times by arrangement. Free. Tel: 0131 229 1142.

An ancient church, the 'West Kirk', was rebuilt by Hippolyte Blanc in 1894.

ST. JOHN'S CHURCH
West end of Princes Street.

All reasonable times. Free.
Tel: 0131 229 7565.

An impressive 19th-century church, the nave of which was built in 1817 by William Burn. There is a fine collection of Victorian stained glass.

ST. MARY'S CATHEDRAL
Palmerston Place, West End.
Mon-Sat 07.30 (morning prayers) 18.15, Sun 08.00-19.00.
Occasionally later in summer. Shop.
Tel: 0131 225 0293.

Built 1879, with the western towers added in 1917. The central spire is 276 feet high and the interior is impressive.

SCOTTISH NATIONAL GALLERY OF MODERN ART
Belford Road.
All year – Mon-Sat 10.00-17.00, Sun 12.00-17.00 (extended hours during Festival). Free. Parking available. Cafe.
Tel: 0131 624 6200. www.natgalscot.ac.uk

Scotland's collection of 20th century painting, sculpture and graphic art, with masterpieces by Derain, Matisse, Braque, Hepworth, Picasso and Giacometti; and work by Hockney, Caulfield and Sol Le Witt. Also Scottish School.

WEST REGISTER HOUSE
West side of Charlotte Square.
Mon-Fri. Exhibitions: 10.00-16.00. Search Room: 09.00-16.45. Free.
Tel: 0131 553 1314.

Formerly St. George's Church, 1811, this now holds the more modern documents of the Scottish Record Office

SOUTHSIDE, TOLLCROSS and MORNINGSIDE

ROYAL OBSERVATORY
Blackford Hill.
Mon-Sat 10.00-1700, Sun, bank holidays 12.00-17.00. Public Observing Oct-Mar Fridays at 7.30pm (Weather permitting). Entrance charge. Parking available. Gift shop.
Tel: 0131 668 8405.

Situated at the home of the Royal Observatory and University Department of Astronomy the Visitor Centre demonstrates the work of astronomers, especially with telescopes in Australia and Hawaii. Also on show is the largest telescope in Scotland.

SCOUT MONUMENT
Valleyfield Street; Tollcross.
Jan-Dec exc. public holidays. Mon-Fri 09.30-16.30. Please call for opening times. Free. Donation Box. Tel: 0131 229 3756.

Based within Area Scout offices, an exhibition of the history of the Scout movement in Edinburgh and worldwide.

EAST END and PORTOBELLO

ARTHUR'S SEAT
Holyrood Park, East of the City Centre.
Entrances at Meadowbank, Holyrood, Dalkeith Road and Duddingston.

Arthur's Seat is the peak of this amazing set of volcanic hills, which are said to make the form of a crouching lion. The volcano would originally have erupted underwater in the Carboniferous Period, greatly forming the shape of the landscape for many miles around. It has been dormant in the region of 335 million years. On the north side are St Margaret's Loch and the ruins of St Anthony's Chapel, and up in the midst of the peaks is Dunsapie Loch. To the Western edge are the impressive Salisbury Crags.

CALTON HILL
Off Regent Road at East end of city centre.
All times. Daylight hours. Free. (City of Edinburgh Council)
Tel: 0131 200 2000.

A city centre hill, 350 feet above sea level, with magnificent views over Edinburgh and the Firth of Forth. The monumental collection on top includes a part reproduction of the Parthenon, intended to commemorate the Scottish dead in the Napoleonic Wars.

EDINBURGH EXPERIENCE
City Observatory, Calton Hill.
Car park at summit; pedestrian access by steps from Regent Road. Early Apr-late Oct. Mon-Sun 10.30-17.00. Other times by arrangement. Entrance Charge. Parking available.
Tel: 0131 556 4365.

20 minute full-colour three-dimensional slide show, viewed through 3-D glasses. The story of Scotland's Capital is told, from its volcanic birth to the present day.

PORTOBELLO
Northeast side of city, on the coast of the Firth of Forth

Portobello's beginnings go back to 1742, when a solitary cottage was built by a survivor of the battle of Puerto Bello. The cottage became a village which was incorporated into Edinburgh in 1896. Most famous as a holiday resort in the early to mid 20th Century, the typical British seaside amenities can still be seen here, with a fairground, games arcades and ice cream sellers populating the beachfront.

LEITH

ROYAL YACHT BRITANNIA

Ocean Terminal, Leith.
Open all year. Admission times April to September are 9.30am –
4.30pm and October to March 10.00am to 3.30pm. (Car parking).
Information: 0131 555 5566

For over forty years *The Royal Yacht Britannia* served the Royal Family,
travelling over one million miles to become the most famous ship in the
world. Travelling to every corner of the globe, in a career spanning 968
Royal and Official visits, she played a leading role in some of the defining
moments of recent history. To Her Majesty The Queen and the Royal
Family, *Britannia* proved to be the perfect Royal residence for glittering
state visits, official receptions, honeymoons and relaxing family holidays. So
as you can imagine this unique vessel has a fascinating story to tell. And
now that she has made Edinburgh's historic port of Leith her final home
you can discover her story for yourself. Follow in the footsteps of Kings and
Queens, Presidents and Prime Ministers and step aboard *The Royal Yacht
Britannia*.

LAMB'S HOUSE

Burgess Street, Leith.
Visits by prior arrangement. (NTS). Tel: 0131 554 3131.

The restored residence and warehouse of Andrew Lamb, a prosperous
merchant of the 17th century. Now an old people's day centre.

OUTSKIRTS

BUTTERFLY AND INSECT WORLD

Dobbies Garden World, 5m S. of Edinburgh on A7 to Dalkeith.
Open all year round exc. Xmas, Boxing Day and New Year 9.30-
17.30 summer 10.00-17.00 winter Entrance charges. Parking
available. Gift shop. Tearoom. Tel: 0131 663 4932.

The farm, housed in a large greenhouse with lush tropical plants, cascading
waterfalls and lily ponds, provides the setting for butterflies from all over
the world to fly freely around.

CANAL CENTRE

Baird Road, Ratho, 8 miles West of Edinburgh, signposted.
Jan-Dec. Charges for use of facilities. Parking available.
Restaurant and bars.
Tel: 0131 333 1320/1251.

Based at the Bridge Inn at Ratho, two luxury canal boat restaurants cruise
the Union Canal.

CRAIGMILLAR CASTLE

A68, 3.5m Southeast of city centre.
Opening standard exc. Oct-Mar closed Thu pm and all day Fri
(winter); Thu pm (summer). Entrance charge.
Tel: 0131 244 3101.

Imposing ruins of massive 14th-century keep enclosed in the early 15th
century by an embattled curtain wall.

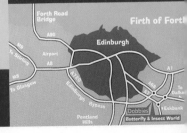

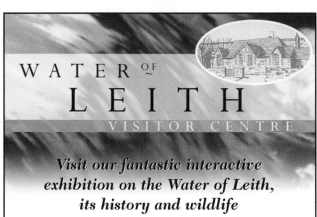

CRAMOND
5m NW of city centre, on the shores of the Firth of Forth.
Parking available.

This picturesque 18th century village is situated at the mouth of the River Almond. Conducted walks around the village start from The Maltings, Jan-Sep, Sun 15.00, free.

CRYSTAL VISITORS CENTRE
Eastfield, Penicuik, 10m South of Edinburgh.
Mon-Sat 10.00-17.00 Sun 11.00-17.00.
Entrance is free – there is a charge for the factory tour.
Treasures of Scotland Gift Shop. Restaurant.
Tel: (01968) 675128.

Factory tours (30 mins) reveal the secrets of glassmaking from glassblowing through cutting to engraving. Extended Activity tours include the chance to try glassblowing and cutting (6-12 persons, booking essential). Children must fit the safety glasses provided. Exhibition and video entitled 'Capturing the Light'. Tour available at weekends from Easter to October.

LAURISTON CASTLE
N. of A90 at Crammond Road South, 4m W/NW of city centre.
Apr-Oct; daily except Fri 11.00-13.00, 14.00-17.00; Nov-Mar - Sat & Sun only 14.00-16.00. Entrance charge. Parking available.
Tel: 0131 336 2060/225 2424, ext. 6682.

The original tower house built by Sir Archibald Napier, father of the inventor of Logarithms was much extended by William Burn in the 1820's

SCOTTISH AGRICULTURAL MUSEUM
Ingliston, nr. Edinburgh Airport.
Mon-Fri 10.00-17.00. Open to groups outside normal hours/season, by arrangement. Parking available. Shops. Tearoom.
Tel: 0131 333 2674.

Scotland's national museum of country life. Farming, old trades and skills, social and home life

WATER OF LEITH VISITOR CENTRE
24 Lanark Road, Slateford
OPEN Every day 10am to 4 pm April to September (Open Wednesday to Sunday October to March) Modest Entrance Charge
Tel: 0131 455 7367 www.waterofleith.edin.org

Experience the drama of river life and discover how to protect it at the fantastic interactive Water of Leith exhibition. Family fun as Edinburgh's watery heritage and wildlife is revealed. You can follow the river's journey along the new Water of Leith Walkway. Starting at Balerno and flowing 12 miles through the capital to Leith, it is a unique way to discover some of Edinburgh's most beautiful places. The Visitor Centre is half way along the walkway on Lanark Road.

shopping

There are two things you will more than likely be intending to take home with you as mementos of your trip to Edinburgh: a bottle of good Malt Whisky and something tartan. You'll find both very easily. In fact, as our favourite Glaswegian Billy Connolly puts it: 'See these wee hairy highlanders in kilts that all the shops have for tourists to take home with them? The Scots must be the only race in the world that buy them and give them to each other!' There are plenty of such shops to be found. However, there is a lot more to be bought in the city if you have the inclination and Edinburgh is a real shopper's heaven if you know where to look. There are designer fashions, excellent quality leather goods, meats and cheeses to die for, great wines, some fantastic unique crafts and great little knickknacks all to be found in the city. So, if what you're after is a day out with your favourite plastic friend, here is our guide to help you max out that credit card for all its worth!

OLD TOWN AND BRIDGES

Forbidden Planet   40-41 South Bridge 558 8226

So what can one buy in a shop named after a bad Sci-Fi flick? Well, how about: American comics; Sci-Fi & Fantasy books, movie magazines, posters, DVD's, videos, t-shirts and cards; toys relating to movies, computer games and superheroes; art books; collectibles; costumes and, well, I think you probably get the picture by now.

Ripping Music & Tickets   91 South Bridge 226 7010

Edinburgh has a lot of good little music shops away from the big boys on Princes Street and this is one of them. A decent selection of current and more unusual stuff, Ripping is mostly known as the place to buy tickets for any gig in Scotland. If you fancy seeing a band while you're here, your best bet is to look at the board in the window to see what's coming up in the near future that they're selling tickets for.

Toskana   21 South Bridge 557 8130

Toskana also have a unit on Princes Street, but I'm mentioning this one for a specific reason. Basically, this is an Italian style leather shop, with leather jackets in all shapes, sizes and colours. I understand they also do a one-day fitting service, but you'll have to check the details with them. The main reason I recommend them is that last year they ran a brilliant ad campaign, by simply writing in their window: 'Mr Toskana is getting divorced – Everything must go!' They ended up with press coverage from the ex-Mrs Toskana claiming the divorce was finalised ages ago and the whole thing was just highly amusing. A top promotional idea and the products are obviously good quality or they wouldn't be expanding the way they are…

The Rusty Zip   14 Teviot Place 226 4634

Everything old is new again. With the retro trend that has overwhelmed the fashion industry since the eighties ended, second hand and retro clothes shops are abounding. This is a pretty good one, but you feel a bit like the clothes are going to consume you as you enter the shop. Aimed at the student market, but perfectly suitable for anyone else wanting to relive their youth – or their parents'!

Deadhead Comics   27 Candlemaker Row 226 2774

Deadhead is the only other comic shop in Edinburgh worth mentioning besides FP, really. They have a pretty good second hand range and most of the American titles, as well as, I believe, some of the less mainstream titles. Worth a browse, if you're into that sort of thing.

Crystal Clear   52 Cockburn Street 226 7888

Spiritualism, crystals, tarot and other matters of the ethereal are all catered to here. Whether it's a book on Native American gods, an energy-focussing piece of Brazilian amethyst or a silver Celtic charm, you'll find it here. Although be warned, it's a small shop and gets quite cramped – claustrophobics beware!

Eden   37 Cockburn Street 220 3372

One of those great shops for buying knickknacks to fill your house with, whether it's a mirror made out of driftwood or a furry candle, you'll find it here. Good place to find little gifts to take home too, I'd have thought!

Enchantment   57 Cockburn Street

If you are even remotely interested in faeries or know someone who is, you have to visit this shop. The windows are absolutely filled with little statues of them in every shape, size and pose. There are also tarot, pagan and Celtic crafts and a small selection of books. But the faeries are really the thing to see.

Fopp   55 Cockburn Street 220 0133

Another little record shop, my brother-in-law reliably informs me that they have by far the best selection of "funky and alternative" stuff. And he would know.

Ground Control   33 Cockburn Street 622 7317

Metal has it's home here, in black and band-themed t-shirts, leather trousers, patches, silver skulls and the like. I think you can even get piercings here to put some of Ground Control's own body jewellery into. There's also an array of smoking paraphernalia in the window that wouldn't look out of place in Amsterdam, which I'm sure is for decorative purposes only…

Lava   47 Cockburn Street

Well, it appears we have located the birthplace of all things kitsch. Lava lamps may have inspired this shop, but it carries a lot more besides, including anything garish and loud, like feather boa picture frames. If it's tacky and loud you're looking for, look no further!

Pie in the Sky   21 Cockburn Street 220 1477

And just to show we hold no bias against any lifestyle choices in Cockburn Street, the hippy movement is alive and well in Pie in the Sky. Clothes-wise it's tie-dyed and hand woven, while you can buy all kinds of smellies in the incense and patchouli oil family, as well as all kinds of earrings and rings. This shop smells like I imagine the sixties must have. Except for Woodstock, obviously…

Whiplash Trash   53 Cockburn Street 226 1005

In case you thought I was kidding about lifestyle choices, we finish Cockburn Street with the less than subtly named Whiplash Trash. Sex and pseudo-sadomasochism are catered for here, so if it's leather basques or crotchless pants you're after, you'll get them here and a lot more besides. Doesn't have the seedy feel of a sex shop, more of a fun atmosphere with clothes and 'marital aids'. Maybe we should rename Cockburn Street 'Little Amsterdam' after all. Just be careful not to mis-pronounce the street name in here…

Mr Wood's Fossils   5 Cowgatehead 220 1344

Stan Wood opened this shop in 1988 after realising there was a market for selling on the many and varied important fossil finds he had made across Scotland. There's now a range of fossils and minerals from all over the world, including items like shark and dinosaur teeth, fossil fish and ammonites. The staff are also very knowledgeable and happy to answer questions. Gives a whole new meaning to the idea of owning a piece of history, doesn't it?

The Cook's Bookshop   118 West Bow 226 4445

One of Clarissa Dixon-Wright's pre-TV fame ventures, The Cook's Bookshop has a book on anything you could imagine about cooking. There are old and new titles, with coverage of all aspects of food and wine for anyone from a professional chef to the average Joe who just likes his food. Or wine, as the case may be…

Transreal Fiction   7 Cowgatehead 226 2822

A bookshop especially for those of a Science Fiction and Fantasy persuasion, the range here covers the above types plus Art, Tattoo Art, Faerie books and the very topical JRR Tolkein. All books are new stock, there is no second hand. There are also little themed calendars and the like, along the same lines. One of the better window displays I've seen, with some really eye-catching artwork on show.

Royal Mile

If you're after anything like a wee hairy Highlander, a shortbread tin, a kilt or anything else tartan, you'll find the lot somewhere in the multitudinous Scottish shops on the Royal Mile. They are all much of the same standard, in my humble opinion, so your best bet is really to browse these types of shops to see what they have and if it is what you're looking for. I won't try to list any of these types of shops here, since the list would be exceptionally long and each entry much the same. What I will do instead is mention some of the shops on the High Street that are a bit more unusual and stray from the blueprint somewhat.

Carson Clark Gallery   181-183 Canongate 556 4710

This place is great, if you're at all interested in history. You can buy antique maps and sea charts here for any part of the world. I've always liked the idea of lining a wall with an old antique style sea chart, but haven't quite managed it yet. Even if you don't want to buy anything, pop in here for a look, some of the maps are absolutely beautiful!

Edinburgh Bear Company   46 High Street 557 9564

It's amazing what you can buy in specialist shops these days. Teddy bears anyone? Selling all variations, one would presume there are a lot of picnics had here. From hand made to manufactured by top brand names, if you can't find the ideal bedtime partner in here, then you're just too fussy.

International Newsagents   351 High Street 225 4827

If you're looking for a newspaper from home to keep up with events while you're away, this is the place to look – if you can get it anywhere in Edinburgh, they'll have it here.

Royal Mile Whiskies   379-381 High Street 225 3383

Ok, two shops here where the clue is in the name. This shop is on the Royal Mile and sells…whisky. Actually, it sells a lot of whisky. So if you want to take a bottle home with you, this is a good bet, where you'll get a wide range to select from and some good advice too. As a point of interest, you should note that there are two spellings of whisky: Scotch Whisky or Irish Whiskey.

The Cigar Box   361 High Street 225 3534

And here's our next literal shopping experience. If you're in the mood to try a taste of Cuba in Edinburgh, here's your spot. There are a few such shops in Edinburgh and this one is quite new but seems, to someone who doesn't smoke, to have a pretty good selection.

The Old Children's Bookshelf   175 Canongate 558 3411

This is one big nostalgia trip to anyone who grew up in the UK or ever read UK published books and comics. It is a treasure trove of youthful memories, with the Beano, Dandy, Eagle, Bunty and every other comic alongside a large range of various children's books by the likes of Enid Blyton, A A Milne and C S Lewis. The collection ranges back over the last century, but predominately covers 1900 to 1970. If there's something in particular you're looking for, ask – they'll try to track it down for you and send it on to your home address when they find it!

The Tappit Hen   89 High Street 557 1852

Amongst the range of jewellers available throughout the Old and New Towns this one doesn't particularly stand out when you see it. It does, however, carry a very unusual range of Celtic jewellery, which is difficult to find anywhere else. For example, my wife and I bought our wedding rings here: a pair of Celtic Moon Rings, which have always drawn comments on how unusual they are. I also only recently found out that my Dad bought my Mum's engagement ring here, a few years back, so a bit of a family tradition, apparently!

Ye Olde Christmas Shoppe   145 Canongate 557 9220

I should own up in advance that I'm a sucker for Christmas, so this shop was a shoe in for a mention. Full of all kinds of more traditional than tacky Christmas decorations and bits and bobs, this place just has a wonderful atmosphere about it. Not quite sure how they manage to stay open all year, and I can only presume that there are people out there who really do wish it could be Christmas every day! (Actually, I'm sure there's one of this type of shop in Amsterdam too. Hmmmm)

Cruise   14 St Mary's Street 556 2532

Used to be extremely popular in the nineties as the place to buy your smart casual clothing. Still worthy of a mention, selling top name brands. Most shops of this type have relocated to the New Town/George Street area, but Cruise continues to be successful here in the heart of the Old Town.

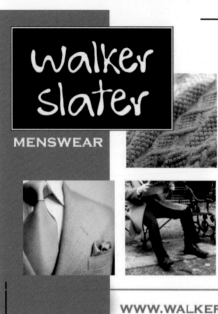

Clarkson's Jewellers 87 West Bow 225 8141

Most of the jewellery here is hand made in their own workshop above the premises and comes with their trademark engraved into it. This is a family run business that has been established for over forty years and produces some really unique pieces worth seeing. Another great place to buy presents if you want something unusual that is exclusively Edinburgh.

Cuttea Sark 26 Victoria Street 226 6245

Ok here's a clever name. The Cutty Sark was a sailing ship, in fact, it was best known as one of the last 'Tea Clippers', that regularly sailed round the Cape of Good Hope to China and brought back tea for us Brits to drink in the 19th Century. She had an adventurous life, including one captain who committed suicide on board. Cuttea Sark has played on this and mixed in the 'tea' into its name and sells a wide range of... coffee. Ok, and tea too, to be fair, but that wouldn't have been at all amusing.

Iain Mellis Cheesemonger 30a Victoria Street 226 6215

One of Edinburgh's favourite sons, Iain Mellis' cheese is renowned in the city. Made traditionally and bought direct from Scottish farms, Iain knows exactly how to look after his cheeses and you are welcome to taste them before you buy. There's goat, sheep and buffalo cheeses as well as the standard cow on offer. You couldn't miss this shop with your eyes closed – the smell is absolutely amazing!

Mackenzie Leather Goods 34 Victoria Street 220 0089

This business started out in the 70's as a saddlery on Arran, where they still have a workshop. Nowadays, they specialise more in leather luggage, bags and briefcases of an extremely high quality and workmanship. Definitely worth popping into if you've got too much to take home in your own cases!

Scottish Gourmet Foods 28 Victoria Street 226 2327

If you want to take home some haggis, black pudding or smoked salmon for your loved ones, there's no better place to buy it than here.

The Old Town Bookshop 8 Victoria Street 225 9237

Right, if you have no idea what I mean by "I love the smell of an old bookshop", then this will be lost on you. If you do, you must visit this little second hand shop. It has a broad range of books and some real gems, if you're prepared to look for them.

The Rolling Stone Gallery 42 Victoria Street 226 7707

This is my favourite shop in Edinburgh. I could happily live here. It smells amazing thanks to the range of scented candles, oils and incense on offer, but there's a lot more too. Hand-made wooden boxes in all shapes and sizes, most with wrought iron decorations, mirrors, candle holders and, of course, Eastern European theatre posters for Shakespeare plays! I rarely pass without stopping in, even if I don't buy anything. No sign of Bill Wyman either, which is a bonus!

Walker Slater 20 Victoria Street 220 2636

Last but not least on Victoria Street is this highly stylish clothes shop. Offering pretty much anything you desire: knitwear, cashmere, tweeds, linens and cloths in the form of made to measure suits, shirts and coats, if you need to dress to impress or want to take home some high quality Scottish clothing, look no further.

NEW TOWN AND STOCKBRIDGE

Most of the shops on Princes Street are fashion related in some way. There are three upmarket national chains doing clothes for men and women, which are:

Gap 131 Princes Street 220 3303

Next 107-108 Princes Street 225 9290

River Island 111 Princes Street 226 3272

Then there are a couple of ladies only fashion shops:

Monsoon 45 Princes Street 558 3544

Which specialises in what I suppose you'd call "pretty" fashion – dresses mostly – and its sister shop:

Accessorize 99a Princes Street 225 8056

Which sells hats, jewellery and scarves etc to go with the Monsoon outfits.

For ladies' shoes there's:
Nine West 99 Princes Street 220 1444

And for men's and ladies' shoes and handbags, there's:

Russell & Bromley 106 Princes Street 225 7444

And for some great quality lingerie, try:

La Senza 117 Princes Street 226 1689

If you don't find anything you want there, then there are several major department stores, notably:

Debenhams 112 Princes Street 225 1320

Jenners 48 Princes Street 225 2442

Trading in the same building since 1838, the grand old dame of Edinburgh, Jenners is great for high quality clothing, shoes, gifts, toys, perfumery – oh anything. Even if you don't buy anything here, you should go in for a wander around anyway – especially if you're here in the run up to Christmas!

Marks & Spencer 45 Princes Street 225 2301

There's one really good Scottish shop for tartan wear etc. on Princes Street, which is:

Romanes & Paterson 62 Princes Street 225 4966

They specialise in tartan, tweed and knitwear, with other little Scottish goodies, like whiskey sample boxes.

Then there's a range of little and not-so little unique shops, like:

Lush 44 Princes Street 557 3177

You'll smell this shop before you see it. They produce a range of handmade, natural soaps and beauty products, with cool little things called "bath bombs" among the novelties on offer

The Body Shop 90a Princes Street 220 6330

A major UK company, The Body Shop is founded on the basis of moral, fair trade with third world countries and natural ingredients, so ladies can spruce themselves up without feeling guilty.

Thornton's 99b Princes Street 225 9335

Mmmmmmmm. Chocolate. And lots of it.

Whittard of Chelsea 23 Princes Street 557 9324

Lots of teas and coffees in all kinds of yummy variations, as well as some rather nice mugs to drink them from.

There are also two major shopping centres at the East End of Princes Street:

St James Centre, right at the East End, where Princes Street meets Leith Street, which has a lot of small versions of the bigger shops on Princes Street, like **Next**, **River Island**, **HMV**, **Top Shop** and **Thornton's**. The biggest thing in there is **John Lewis**, a major department store with perfumery, clothes, home wares and the like, which has the operating slogan 'Never knowingly undersold'. There's also a decent sized food court upstairs.

Princes Mall is at the East End on top of Waverley Train Station. In here are some more unique shops, like **Coda Music**, **Benetton** and a few other various clothes retailers. There's an interesting and educational Science shop for kids and a great little sweet shop on the ground floor, next to a massive Food Court, which is a good place to stop for a bite during any frenetic shopping.

The other major shopping street in the area is **George Street**, which has a different ethos entirely. Not the high street retailers, but the more exclusive, upmarket shops are to be found here. Jewellers, ladies' fashion and gentlemen's attire are all to be found here.

To begin with, let's cover the ladies' shops, since they are definitely the dominant species here:

Firstly there's:

French Connection 68-70 George Street 220 1276

There's always an exception to the rule, isn't there? This is the only High Street retailer here, which is fine because it's really trying to position itself upmarket anyway.

Other than FCUK, there's a plethora of ladies' outlets, many of the type where the gents can have a comfy seat and a cup of coffee while their good lady wives try to max the credit card:

Coast 61 George Street 225 9190

Escada 35a George Street 225 9885

Hobbs 47 George Street 220 5386

Jigsaw 49 George Street 225 4501

Karen Millen 53 George Street 220 1589

Phase Eight 47b George Street 226 4009

Viyella 34 George Street 225 4652

There's also one store that has a particular speciality – the clue is in the name:

The Cashmere Store 67 George Street 226 4861

Then there's 'something for the gentleman', with a few men's stores selling suits etc, and a few of them offering their own tailoring services too:

Austin Reed 39 George Street 225 6703

Crombie 63 George Street 226 1612

FARLOWS

AHEAD OF THE FIELD FOR OVER 160 YEARS

COUNTRY CLOTHING, FISHING TACKLE, SHOOTING ACCESSORIES

58 GEORGE STREET, EDINBURGH EH2 2LR TEL: 0131 225 7225. WWW.FARLOWS.CO.UK

TAX FREE FOR TOURISTS

Cruise   94 George Street 226 3524

This is currently a unisex shop, but at time of writing I understand it is about to become a men's store, as they open a four floor ladies' store on Castle Street.

Jigsaw Menswear   103 George Street 226 7362

George Street also caters to the ladies' other needs with a number of jewellers. The big boys are:

Hamilton & Inches   87 George Street 225 4898

Lime Blue Diamond Store   107 George Street 220 2164

Mappin & Webb   88 George Street 225 5502

And, just to be complete, there are a few apothecaries/perfumeries, which seem to have suddenly become quite popular, when I wasn't looking:

Jo Malone   93 George Street 478 8555

Penhaligon's   33 George Street 220 3210

Space NK   97-103 George Street 225 6371

At the end of all that, there are three shops that can find you relief from a day's heavy retail therapy:

The Pier   104 George Street 226 3415

Mostly sells furniture and such downstairs, but also has the most amazing range of scented candles.

Sportfish   58 George Street 225 7225

If you feel you just need to get away from it all, pop in here for any outdoor clothing or equipment needs and some good advice on where to go, too.

Justerini & Brooks   45 George Street 226 4202

And if it's all just too much and your only solace is likely to be in a bottle of grape juice, then the world famous Justerini & Brooks are guaranteed to have a bottle to please your senses as much as it removes the day's stresses!

While Rose Street is most well known for its pubs, there are a couple of little shops worth visiting there. Firstly, two specialist jewellers:

Argentium Jewellery   105 Rose Street 225 8057

Specialises in some pretty funky modern designs using primarily silver.

The Ringmaker   76 Rose Street 225 7722

Three other nice little outlets are:

Arran Aromatics   105 Rose Street 225 8057

Offer a wide range of bath and body products, handmade soaps and scented candles.

Romulus   136 Rose Street 226 5269

This is just a totally fun shop, with board games, gag presents, lava lamps, t-shirts, mugs and, one special item you may want to pick up while you're here: the Edinburgh edition of Monopoly!

Rana   89 Rose Street 220 2222

I deliberately left this one to last on this street, as it runs a close second in my favourite Edinburgh shops list. Wonderful furniture here, with a South American/Mexican theme – I could furnish three houses happily from this company. If you can't transport such large items home with you, they also have some beautiful glasses, jewellery and other bits and bobs. Careful not to forget to leave, this place is quite absorbing, if smaller than its previous Princes Street incarnation.

As mentioned elsewhere, Thistle Street is a bit of a gem for everything, and it has a couple of very good shops worth visiting:

Jane Davidson   52 Thistle Street 225 3280

Since 1969 this little outlet has been a gem in Edinburgh, selling the best in women's fashion and accessories. They have exclusive Edinburgh rights to sell many top names, such as Diane von Furstenburg, Joop! and Clements Ribiero.

Joseph H Bonnar   72 Thistle Street 226 2811

Another business successfully trading since the sixties, Joseph Bonnar now stocks Scotland's largest range of antique jewellery, selected silver and objects of vertu as well as some of the world's 'rarest and finest' gems.

In honesty, there's not much on Queen Street apart from offices and the occasional pub or restaurant, however, there are a couple of specialist shops worth noting:

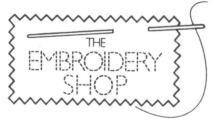

Hein Gericke   60 Queen Street 220 4156

I don't know much about motorcycles, but from what I do know, if you need a motorcycle accessory of any sort, this is the best place to get it from, bar none.

Stewart Christie & Co   63 Queen Street 225 6639

Established in 1792, the same family have been outfitting Scots for over three generations. Bespoke tailors making clothes on the premises, they provide a range of traditional clothing for both country and city including Scottish tweed jackets, English suits, plus two's, cord and moleskin trousers as well as highland dress and tartan evening trousers.

On the remaining cross streets, there are:

Crabtree & Evelyn   4 Hanover Street 226 2478

Very upmarket soap shop, selling lots of lovely smellies and bath products.

Wax Lyrical   3-5 Hanover Street 226 4420

Great candle shop – lots of standards and usually some seasonal favourites: Halloween candles, Valentines Day candles and the like.

Cecil Gee Menswear   3 Frederick Street 225 1418

For the youthful, fashionable, professional male, with suits by the likes of Hugo Boss.

Dickson & MacNaughton   21 Frederick Street 225 4218

Suppliers of country wear and field sports accessories.

Ede & Ravenscroft   46 Frederick Street 225 6354

Classic and modern menswear with both personal tailoring and bespoke tailoring. Also sell shoes and "gentlemen's accessories" Most famous for supplying gowns for graduations and the legal profession.

Electronics Boutique   10 Frederick Street 343 3555

Lots of boy's toys here. My brother-in-law informs me this is the best place in town to buy computer games, and I trust him on that too.

Laing the Jeweller   29 Frederick Street 225 4513

This is the shop I saw a watch going for something like £4,000 in the window. So, if you really, really need to know what time it is…

Oasis   14-16 Frederick Street 225 4624

In my humble experience (i.e. being dragged round the shops on a Saturday), Oasis has some decent items for the fashionable young woman at inexpensive High Street prices. (I'm starting to sound like a catalogue, aren't I?)

Past Times   7a Frederick Street 225 5853

This company is kind of our nemesis, in that, being called 'Pastime Publications', we often get phone calls intended for them. And vice versa, probably. Anyway, this is a pretty cool shop selling bits and pieces modelled on various historical periods. If you're at all a history buff, it's worth checking out.

Schuh   6-6a Frederick Street 220 0290

"Fashion for your feet" is how they brand themselves. This is a bigger branch of the shop that also resides on North Bridge. Trendy shoes, basically – Dr Martens, CAT and the like, for both men and women. And some interesting knee high leather boots.

High & Mighty   4 Castle Street 226 6254

At 6'3", I'm tall enough to be outfitted here, but despite my best efforts of beer drinking and chip eating, I didn't quite manage the girth. A great shop though, with some excellent suits and jackets for men who find that the usual High Street sizes barely fit around one leg…

Thomas Pink   32a Castle Street 225 4264

Thomas Pink shirts are generally accepted as being among the best you can have, so they're not cheap, but they do live up to the hype. This little men's shop got a big sister across the road recently and moved into selling ladies the same quality of clothing too. Fashion plus quality, basically.

Crombie's of Edinburgh   97-101 Broughton Street 557 0111

A great big butcher's and deli at the bottom of the street, Crombie's is very famous for one thing in particular: its sausages. And justifiably so – if you have any cooking facilities while you're here, or can take them home safely – you have to try these…

Villeneuve Wines   49a Broughton Street 558 8441

This is my own personal favourite wine shop. Great selection - they have a policy that all the staff have to try every wine they stock and if even one of them doesn't rate it, it doesn't get stocked. They're also extremely friendly and happy to chat about what you're buying or offer advice. Very nice people.

Geraldine's of Edinburgh   35a Dundas Street 556 4295

Since 1984 Geraldine has been making and selling porcelain dolls and teddy bears. But that's not all, she's also got, wait for it…a teddy bears' and dolls' hospital! How good is that? 25 years ago I'd have thought that was brilliant and frankly I'm still a little excited about it!

Edinburgh Floatarium   29 North West Circus Place 225 3350

Alternative treatment heaven – you can get all kinds of massages here, float in a sensory deprivation tank, or buy essential oils, candles, crystals or incense.

Iain Mellis Cheesemonger   6 Bakers Place 225 6566

Yes, it's another branch of our purveyor of smelly milk products. In fact, I think this might be the original one, but don't quote me on that. See Victoria Street write up for more info.

Kathleen Dickens   13 Raeburn Place 343 3555

Another good ladies' fashion shop, in the heart of Stockbridge.

Montresor   35 St Stephen Street 220 6877

Seems to be absolutely full of all kinds of antique and costume jewellery and the like – the kinds of things people would, one supposes, treasure if they had them locked away in a box or in the attic. Looks like the range here could just about stretch to anything!

Tinies   8 St Stephen Street 226 6228

I wouldn't have believed there was a shop anywhere in the world that specialised in selling tiny porcelain animals. Apparently, I was wrong. Which is not necessarily a bad thing! If that's what you're into – there's a fine selection here.

WEST END AND LOTHIAN ROAD

First XV   6 Haymarket Terrace 337 4746

Just down the road from Murrayfield, you might not be surprised to find a sports shop selling everything to do with "The Hard Game". Focusing on rugby union, rather than league, you can get everything here from boots right up to replica tops of your team, including balls and all. So if you've arrived in Edinburgh for a game and realised you've left your kit at home, panic ye not, you can totally re-stock here…

Hugh MacPherson   17 West Maitland Street 225 4008

A very well respected Scottish formal wear shop, with one of the biggest ranges of kilts for hire available in the city. If you need a kilt, or, hell, just fancy wearing a kilt to something while you're here, this is a good bet…

Wonderland Toys   97 Lothian Road 229 6428

I love to see old-fashioned shops thriving in the face of modern megastores, and I'm delighted that this little shop is still going. Specialising in trains and models, they sell more traditional toys and I have a particularly fond spot for this place. It seemed slightly magical to me as a boy and I'm pleased to say there's still a little touch of that every time I go past.

Studio One Gallery   10 Stafford Street 226 5812

An amazing array of crafts and all sorts on sale here – they also put on exhibitions of lesser-known artists work. Another that's definitely worth a browse while you're in town.

Fraser's   145 Princes Street 225 2472

Trading since 1921 at this location, Fraser's is another of the big hitting department stores on Princes Street. They offer clothing for men and women, perfumes and cosmetics, home wares and bed linen etc and even a personal shopper service, should you need one.

SOUTHSIDE, TOLLCROSS AND MORNINGSIDE

Till's Bookshop   1 Hope Park Crescent 667 0895

Since 1986 Richard and Ann Till have been running this great little bookshop just off the Meadows. They specialise in literature, SF, mystery and show business and I believe also carry stock of original old movie posters. Had to include this on the basis that a film buff and bibliophile friend of mine insists it is the best bookshop in Edinburgh.

Majestic Wine Warehouse   39 Causewayside 662 8512

This is not for popping in for a bottle, as they only sell by the case, but my wine-quaffing colleague tells me he absolutely guarantees that this is the place to find some truly excellent wines at much better prices than they should be. So if you've got the car and want to take some bottles back with you…

Miller's Antiques   187-189 Causewayside 662 1429

I'm not really an antiquer, but the wooden furniture in the window of this shop has always looked impressive to me and I was very much sold when I saw they sell old-fashioned footballs with clubs' names printed on them – fantastic!

The Meadows Pottery   11a Summerhall Place 662 4064

The vases and other pottery in the window here are unusual and unique. Everything is made on the premises and has been since 1988. They describe their wares as 'domestic and decorative stoneware', which seems fair to me – and they'll even undertake a commission, should you have something particular in mind that you just can't find for sale.

Art et Facts

19 Roseburn Terrace Edinburgh EH12 5NG

Telephone 0131 346 7730

ESTABLISHED 1989

Ten minutes walk from Princes Street will bring you to Art et Facts. We have a huge selection of prints and originals by some of the top artists in the UK. Floral, landscape, golf and maritime art to name but a few.

Well worth a visit open 6 days from 10am to 5pm. You can also visit our Website at **www.picturesonnet.com**, we will also happily arrange mailing to your home.

Love is such a beautiful thing
signed original monotype etchings by Simon Bull, long considered the UKs leading contemporary artist

The Letter
signed limited edition prints by Jack Vettriano, Britains foremost contemporary narrative painter

The artists studio, Dundee
signed limited edition prints by James McIntosh Patrick, widely regarded as one of the finest Scottish Landscape painters of the 20th century, maintaining his position as Scotlands most collectable artist

Decon Brodies Tavern
signed prints, limited editions and originals by Lynn Hanley. Lynn's paintings, full of characters and quirky details give her work a unique character all of its own, the Old Town and vibrant life of Edinburgh her main inspiration

Backbeat Records 31 East Crosscauseway 668 2666

There are several good little second hand record shops up here worth browsing and this is definitely one of them. They specialise in blues, folk, jazz, soul and reggae. Successfully running a little business like this since 1981 suggests they have staying power, too.

Edinburgh Coin Shop 11 West Crosscauseway 668 2928

One for the collectors among you, here is a little shop that since 1977 has been offering coins, medals, cigarette cards, stamps and postal history. They also have auctions five or six times a year, so ring to se if there's likely to be one while you're in town.

Alligator 4 Nicolson Street 556 3322

A cool and slightly funky gift and knickknack shop. Lots of bright colours. Sadly, as seems to be the case with places around here, promises alligators, but doesn't deliver.

Southside Books 58 South Bridge 558 9009

Another good second hand bookshop. My lovely wife bought me a beautiful old leather-bound copy of Wuthering Heights from here that has pride of place on the bookcase. Thus, this shop merits special mention.

F&D Simpson 28-30 West Preston Street 667 3058

Another outdoor specialist shop, they've got all the gear you could need, especially if you're thinking of doing a spot of fishing while you're here. Which apparently you can do up on Dunsapie Loch on Arthur's Seat – but don't quote me on that!

Professor Plastic 15a West Richmond Street 622 7168

Yes, it's another record shop, but this one has particular speciality for LP's. So if you, like me, know someone who's a bit of a vinyl freak, here's your perfect shop for an unusual holiday pressie.

Cameron Toll shopping centre is right at the South end of Dalkeith Road. It has a massive Food Supermarket, but also quite a few clothing shops, including **The Officers Club** and **Dorothy Perkins**, a couple of sports shops, a **Thornton's**, an **Our Price** music store and an **Ottakar's** book store among others. If you're down this end of town anyway, it's worth popping in, and they've also got a food court if you want to have lunch or coffee in the middle of your shop.

Baloo 117 Bruntsfield Place 229 4006

Being in the in-between stage, where I'm not a kid and not yet a parent, I have no real excuse to go to places like this little toy shop, except for my various 'nieces' and 'nephews' birthdays, which is simply not often enough…

Everyone's Designs 213 Bruntsfield Place 447 1504

I should mention there's a lot of kid shops up here. Witness this gift shop that specialises in…Winnie the Pooh.

Nippers & Flippers 139 Bruntsfield Place 229 4111

These are actually two separate shops just next to each other, but connected. Nippers is a great clothes shop for wee ones, while Flippers is their equivalent in a shoe shop! Again, don't need to shop here myself yet, but in a few years' time..?

Iain Mellis Cheesemonger 205 Bruntsfield Place 447 8889

Good Lord, even I didn't realise there were so many of these around Edinburgh. It's another outlet for Edinburgh's top cheese-seller.

Fool Clothing 308 Morningside Road 447 1040

An alternative clothes store, this is for people who like to dress colourfully and baggily – thus the "fool", as in jester, who represents the style. Used to have a shop on Nicolson Street too, but this is their only outlet now.

One Step Ahead 177 Morningside Road 447 0999

This is a high quality outdoor sports shop, but not outdoor as in hunting and shooting, more like jogging, cycling and rollerblading. They also have a great juniors range if you have kids to outfit too. See, I told you they cater well for kids out here!

Out of the Blue 177 Morningside Road 446 9900

This is a little gift shop I'd never heard of until I was out and about researching this guide, and I ended up going in and buying a present for my wife of a handy little metal contact lenses travel case. They also do things like lava lamps, little pewter statues from pop cultural phenomenons like The Simpsons and Lord of the Rings and such like.

The Fairy Shop Ltd 37-39 Morningside Road 466 7474

Go on, have a guess what kinds of things they sell here. I must say though, I thought if anywhere would have a shop that sold actual fairies, Morningside would be it. Sadly not. They must hide just as well out here as they do in town.

EAST END

Au Naturale Unit 6, Meadowbank Retail Park 661 9006

This is a very large branch of the interiors store, with a great range of extremely reasonable bits and bob for around the house and quirky little gift ideas. Good stock in particular of candles, glassware and crockery, cushions and rugs all at very low prices.

Famous Brunswick Warehouse
Unit 8, Meadowbank Retail Park 652 2885

Shoes in all shapes and sizes, they're stacked up on the racks and the rule is, if they've got them, they're on the shelf and it's all self-service. This allows them to sell some great quality shoes and often some top names like Fila and Cat at much lower prices than you'd pay on the High Street. It's a bit potluck at times, but you can be lucky and find some great bargains.

TK Maxx
Unit 10, Meadowbank Retail Park 661 6611

Speaking of potluck, this place is great. They have all kinds of designer label clothes at absolutely bargain prices – I got a leather jacket worth £250 for £100, for example. You've got to be prepared to browse, because again it is a case of if they've got it, its on the rack.

Valvona & Crolla
19 Elm Row 556 6066

This is an absolutely legendary Italian food and wine shop. If you have any love for Italian food, or fancy cooking yourself something from the land of the lira while you're in Edinburgh, you absolutely have to buy your ingredients here. In fact, make sure you arrive early, because their selection of Italian breads goes down in stock by the end of the day, as it's all fresh. And if you don't have cooking facilities and just want to sample something, they have a little café/restaurant in the back, which is also worth visiting.

Vinyl Villains
5 Elm Row 558 1170

This is the second hand record shop that used to provide me with spare cash during my summer holidays at home from University, when I was so poor that I had to start selling my old tapes just to go out for a drink of a night. They have a big range of such second hand stuff and it's worth browsing through to see what's there, or even just looking in their window, which is generally adorned with covers of old albums that they've got in stock.

LEITH

Flux Scottish Artisans Gallery
55 Bernard Street 554 4075

A rather nifty little shop just off The Shore, Flux is also a good worthy cause, as it supports the work of all kinds of Scottish artisans by giving them an outlet to retail their work. Successfully trading since 1997, they sell all kinds of unusual things, I always remember a rather cool looking stained glass lamp in the window, that catches my eye every time I pass. There's also cards and gifts – ah, just go in and have a browse, it's that kind of shop.

Graham Tiso
41 Commercial Street 554 0804

If you're intending to go out and see some of the Highlands and glens while you're here, but you've forgotten something, don't worry; this massive warehouse of a shop will have whatever you need. Whether you're going hill walking, mountaineering, camping, canoeing, rock or ice climbing, you'll find everything you need in here, plus some pretty good service, in my experience.

The Pipe Shop
92 Leith Walk 553 3561

Now, I'm not encouraging anyone to take up smoking, just so you understand. However, most of the smokers I know who've ever lived in or near Leith have a tale to tell about this shop. Whether it's: 'I remember the wee guy who runs it from the 80's – he was always dead friendly' or 'I got into smoking this particular French tobacco and this was the only place I could find it', they all seem to have something good to say about it. So that can't be all bad. These days they offer a range of cigarette and pipe tobacco, pipes, lighters, cigars, alternative pipes and accessories. I get the feeling they would have even more on sale if the government moved ahead with plans to legalise cannabis in the coming years…

The Leith Gallery
65 The Shore 553 5255

If you're interested in collecting artwork, this is a great little gallery, displaying some established and many up and coming Scottish artists. I rarely fail to stop and stare in at the new exhibitions here as they come up and they're very much worth a look while you're here. You could find yourself with the perfect thing to make your living room look complete – and what a unique thing to be able to take home!

Ocean Terminal is the real focus of shopping in Leith now and there's a nice range of brand new shops down here. The bonus is that, because it's new, it's not nearly as busy as the places in town, so if you're one of those who like to avoid the crush, this is your ideal solution. There are new units being announced all the time and, at time of writing, I believe **HMV** is the latest to be added. Among those already in place are: **Adams**, a great kids clothes shop; **Au Naturale**; **BHS**, a traditional big department store; **Body Shop**; **Debenhams**; **Gap**; **Logo**; and **S3**, a shop specialising in surf, skate and ski wear.

eating out

When it comes to restaurants, it is hard to argue that any city in Britain can compete with London. However, once I sat down to think about it, my own impression of how many excellent and varied options we Edinburghers have for satisfying our culinary desires is really quite something, and I'd be surprised to see it bettered outside of London on this isle.

While we do lean towards a large number of Italians, thanks to our substantial Italian community, you can also find the varieties of Chinese, Thai, Mexican, Spanish, French, Indian, Mediterranean and African cuisines on offer alongside the International, Fusion and proudly Scottish venues on offer.

In fact, I find it impossible to believe that there is a palate that cannot be satisfied in Edinburgh. And variety is not all we have, there's a wealth of quality to be had as well, with some great, award winning chefs plying their trade in Edinburgh's kitchens and offering up their imaginative visions of food which will undoubtedly make your taste buds tingle.

Whatever it is you're looking for, it is almost certainly available in Edinburgh, and here is our guide to help you track it down, so that you don't have to rely on your nose alone.

OLD TOWN AND BRIDGES

North Bridge Brasserie   20 North Bridge   556 5565

Part of the impressive new Scotsman Hotel, the Brasserie is a welcome addition to Edinburgh's culinary community. The room in which the Restaurant is set is the old entrance to the building – it is light, open and elegant, punctuated with primary colours here and there and with some rather unusual artwork on the walls. The menu has some pretty staple British cuisine, but it is very well done and presented, and there's a fine wine list too. The whole place surrounds a central bar, so the drinks options are not limited to wine.

Pizza Express   23 North Bridge   557 6411

Pizza Express have only just started advertising after over thirty years in business. The reason they've survived until now is that, basically, they're very good at what they do. That is, a quality range of stone-bake style pizzas in an upmarket venue. This is pretty much the king of the pizza venue, forget your Pizza Huts etc, if you want a good meal out rather than just a bite to eat, this is the place. They don't do much other than pizzas, but as a starter, I very much recommend the garlic dough balls.

Negociants
45-47 Lothian Street   225 6313

Long known as one of the "cool" places to sit outside, drink hot chocolate and eat nachos, Negociants has found that many places have copied its template of late, but it was one of the first in Edinburgh. With a good selection of what have become standard these days – steaks and fajitas, for example, followed by any of a range of fresh baked pastries, it's a good place to eat, but also to be seen. Which is pretty much what a lot of the clientele are here for, and they move downstairs to the relaxed, Moroccan style club later on…

Biblos
1a Chambers Street   226 7177

Formerly a pretty decent little café, Biblos only joined us very recently. Beautifully re-decorated and moved a good few rungs upmarket, this is now a very trendy place to be. Decorated in brick and wood, with an overhanging balcony, the clientele mainly consists of students and young professionals. They open early for breakfast and do takeaway on their range of coffees and rolls, for those who didn't manage a bite before they left the house. The rest of the menu consists of wraps, hot sandwiches, salads and a few mains with an international range – curry to pasta and much in between. A good place for lunch, but later it's more of a bar, with a DJ on every night of the week.

The Tower
Museum of Scotland, Chambers Street   225 3003

If I tell you that The Tower has been listed in the Michelin Guide and been awarded the Wine Spectator Award of Excellence, that might be all you'd need to visit this modern and elegant, yet still comfortable restaurant atop the Museum of Scotland's fantastic new building. The menu is made up from the best of Scottish ingredients, like Scottish Rock Oysters, Shetland Salmon and Aberdeen Angus Steaks, with a choice of over 150 wines from all over the world to complement the food. If you're feeling particularly celebratory, you could even indulge in a £1500 bottle of champagne – I personally have yet to have quite that good a day.

If you're interested in star spotting, there's a clutch of British celebrities who have all been and said some very complimentary things about the Tower, so you never know who might be at the next table.

Dial
44-46 George IV Bridge   225 7179

I had the pleasure of bumping into Dial's owner one night out on the town, and was pleased to discover that he's running this great nouvelle cuisine little restaurant more for the joy of it than anything else. And a fine job he's doing too, with modern, interesting options on the menu and a pure white décor, this is a great place to go for a special meal for two, if you're aiming to impress. The staff are very friendly, helpful and happy to chat, if they're not too busy.

The Elephant House
21 George IV Bridge   220 5355

An Edinburgh institution, the Elephant House is pretty much loved by all. Attracting a studenty/intellectual crowd (unsurprising this close to the University), it has a huge back room with an eclectic array of different, salvaged wooden tables that give it a unique charm. The menu ranges from coffees and teas to sandwiches, paninis and full scale, casual meals like fajitas and pizzas. Whatever you're after, if you need to get off your feet and refuel, you'll probably find something here to tempt you. By the way, there are no actual elephants, in case you wondered.

Jackson's
209 High Street   225 1793

Set in a basement off the high street, Jackson's is a very Scottish restaurant. So traditional it is, in fact, that they're keeping the Auld Alliance intact by introducing a touch of the Gallic into their menu. The main staple here is game and you'll notice that not only on the menu, but on the walls as well. Expensive, but very good, if you want to try the best of Scotland's produce in a slightly more "authentic" atmosphere, this is not a bad bet.

Le Sept
7 Old Fishmarket Close   225 5428

A great combination of France and Edinburgh, Le Sept is 'set' in one of the unique little closes running down off the High Street. Considering the address, you won't be surprised to hear that there's fish on the menu, but that's not all. This little gem has been trading successfully since 1982 on the premise that if you provide good food, inexpensively in a nice, unusual setting, you will be successful. As with many of the High Street set, seating is available outside when the weather permits, which is a treat.

Iggs Restaurante
15 Jeffrey Street   557 8184

Iggs is an award winning restaurant. The fayre is a mix of Spanish and Scottish. Is anyone else seeing a pattern developing here? Actually Iggs does an excellent fusion of the two cultures' cuisines and deserves its awards. Iggy Campos has been running this little gem for years now, and he's got a great formula, which works well.

The Reform
267 Canongate   558 9992

One for those who like classy, intimate surroundings, freshly prepared food and a menu with many different options and combinations to make your mouth water. A modern menu in an atmospheric old stone building, The Reform offers good food with imagination. For example, doesn't warm white bean dip, toasted pitta and sea salt roasted vegetables on the same page as pan seared scallops with a margarita sauce with wilted greens and potato rosti really make you want to know what else is also on offer? Unusually for a restaurant with such an exclusive little menu, there are usually at least two or three good, different veggie options, too. But worry not carnivores, there's plenty of meat too…

The Witchery by the Castle   352 Castlehill   225 5613

If every city has a signature restaurant, The Witchery is Edinburgh's. It is difficult not to wax lyrical when describing this unique restaurant. With two separate dining rooms, you can choose either the grand gothic splendour of the main dining room or the intimate, magical ambience of the secret garden. Either one is a real treat. The food is excellent, without exception. What really makes this our flagship, though, is that The Witchery captures all aspects of Edinburgh: Our buildings full of history and stories, our gothic, ghoulish past (the Witchery Tour also starts from here) and our high standards of culinary and service excellence. It's difficult to say enough good things about this dramatic eatery, so I'll stop now, before I become a gibbering sycophant. Just try it for yourself – trust me. And if you're having too much fun to leave, you could book a night in the Inner Sanctum or The Old Rectory, two lavishly decadent suites available for hire upstairs, available with or without ghosts, I presume…

Bann's Vegetarian Café   5 Hunter Square   226 1112

OK, word of forewarning: news has reached me, at time of writing, that this has been sold, so it may be in new hands by the time you read this – however, if it's still there, you should visit arguably the best veggie venue in Edinburgh. A great variety of dishes shows you don't have to be boring to eat meatless, which is good when your wife's a veggie and you're not! They also do great freshly made fruit drinks, which I thoroughly recommend for a cleansing of the body and soul!

Creelers   3 Hunter Square   220 4447

When a seafood restaurant owns its own boat and smokehouse, that can't be a bad thing. It does of course mean that they can't blame "the suppliers", but then they should have no need to! Creelers was established 12 years ago up on the beautiful Isle of Arran. As you would guess, the menu is mainly fresh fish, but there's always at least one veggie and one meat option for those not of an aquatic persuasion. Just been through a refurbishment and looking great for it, this is a great, relaxed place if you're in the seafood mood.

Doric Tavern   15-16 Market Street   225 1084

This could well be the most obliging restaurant in Edinburgh. Already a lovely, comfortable venue done in wood and warm orange tones, with a cosy little wine bar appended next door, the great standard of food would be enough to make this place thoroughly recommendable already. Add to that some incredibly friendly staff and the fact that they are delighted to discuss local history with you over appetisers. Then top it off with the fact that, if you particularly fancy something that's not on the menu, and they can make it, they will! It even says so on the menu! Got quite excited by this on my first visit, but had no need to use that option as it took us an age to pick from what was already on offer. Still, nice to be asked, isn't it?

Grain Store   30 Victoria Street   225 7635

Upstairs on my favourite Edinburgh street lies a little restaurant that is perfect for an intimate meal. Set in some old stone vaulted store rooms, the atmosphere is tangible. Add to this the fact that owners Carlo Coxon and Paul McPhail are personally on the premises as chef and manager respectively, and the high quality dishes, cooked to order from local produce, and you'll see why this restaurant is worth a visit, whether it's a romantic interlude or just a damn good meal you're after.

Howie's   10-14 Victoria Street   225 1721

Howie's seem to have taken over the world, or at least Edinburgh, since the demise of Pierre Victoire. There are several of them around Edinburgh, but I suppose that's because they have a good formula that works well. Modern, smart décor, good service and a good, rotating set menu at not too ridiculous prices. Often used for business meals and a good place to go in a group of any size.

Point Restaurant   34 Bread Street   221 5555

Well, if ever an architect wanted to find his ideal dining place, this would be it. Set in the immense new Point Hotel, with it's glass walls, mirrors and panels, this restaurant would be a shoe-in for the style over content critique – but the food is better than that. Adding a "pan-European" feel to good Scottish cuisine, they've come up with stylish food to match the building – no mean feat! For example: Gylas of Scotch Beef, enhanced with Red Wine and topped with white truffle and potato mash. And very reasonably under £13 for three courses - not to be sniffed at! One of the relatively few hotel restaurants worthy of a visit whether you're staying there or not!

NEW TOWN AND STOCKBRIDGE

Bellini   8b Abercromby Place   476 2602

This is a cracker to start off the New Town. Chef and Partner Angelo Cimini studied catering at Villa St Maria (est. 1290!) and began his career in Venice before moving to Scotland. He is thus hugely qualified to provide this menu, which offers "authentic Italian regional cooking". There's little pasta and no pizza here – instead it's meats and vegetables in all variations of preparations and sauces. A proper Italian culinary experience.

Haldanes   39a Albany Street   556 8407

Mr & Mrs Kelso brought their country house hotel atmosphere to Edinburgh in 1997, and we're very grateful to them for it. Here you'll get good, high quality, stick to your ribs Scottish food in front of a roaring open fire. There's also a seductive array of homemade desserts to look forward to throughout the meal, and a cosy lounge to, well, lounge in while you wait for your table. A real soul-warming experience.

The Basement   10a-12a Broughton Street   557 0097

This is another of my personal favourites, but I couldn't love it nearly as much as my mum does. A great little bar / restaurant with burritos always on the menu, The Basement does all kinds of stuff during the week, including a fair bit of Thai on Wednesday and exclusively Mexican at the weekend. The prices are extremely fair and the food is much better than just 'pub grub'. The Margaritas are also pretty good, whether frozen or on the rocks. The décor is also worth mentioning: bold Latin colours on the walls are complemented by candlelight from the most amazing candleholders, which look to be some part of a car engine, bolted to each table. Book for lunch or dinner, it gets busy!

Oloroso   33 Castle Street   226 7614

Best described as 'London in Edinburgh', Oloroso is the bright new pretender to the throne of best restaurant in Edinburgh. It is the classic, modern New Town to the Witchery's Old Town charm. Elegant, upmarket, full of life and not at all cheap, I can honestly say I had the best steak of my life here only a few months ago. Thoroughly enjoyable, there's even an adjoining bar to adjourn to for an after dinner liqueur. Or a Drambuie, as I call it. There are also great views out over Edinburgh, as it's a rooftop – don't worry though, there's a lift to get you there!

Stac Polly   29-33 Dublin Street   556 2231

Named after a great craggy Scottish Mountain, this very Scottish restaurant has a lot to live up to. And live up it does, with the best of Scottish ingredients combined in traditional and modern ways to give you some unique taste experiences. If you're a bit afraid of trying haggis from the local chippy for example, try the haggis in filo pastry with sweet plum sauce here instead - a much gentler way to break in the taste buds!

Kweilin   19-21 Dundas Street   557 1875

Well, it's a damn fine Cantonese at last! Great food, particularly good fish. The standard is not to just overload the meal with MSG and oil, like some Oriental restaurants, but to prepare it well and serve it well too. There's also a fine wine list and a good selection of malts for afters. All in all, if you're feeling a little more rice than pasta, this is where you wanna be.

Duck's at Le Marche Noir   2-4 Eyre Place   558 1608

Malcolm Duck is a bit of a cult figure in Edinburgh eating circles and until recently, he always appeared personally in photos promoting Duck's. He's rightly proud of his eponymous restaurant and who could blame him? Beautiful, elegant surroundings, an excellent wine list, good food and good service – all in all, you are well and truly spoiled here, and it's an experience to have if you can. The menu, as is

Hard Rock CAFE ®

EDINBURGH

RESTAURANT AND BAR OPEN 12PM – 1AM   RETAIL STORE OPEN 9AM – LATE

AMERICAN MENU INCLUDING VEGETARIAN DISHES

LARGE GROUPS CATERED FOR • CHILDREN WELCOME
(under 14s until 8pm due to local licensing laws)

SPECIAL MENU NOW AVAILABLE • ACCESS FOR DISABLED DINERS

0131 260 3000

HARD ROCK CAFE • EDINBURGH
20 GEORGE STREET, EDINBURGH EH2 2PF

becoming the standard more and more, is brief, with only a few choices per course, but they're freshly prepared to a very high standard. Quality over quantity, basically. You may want to notify them in advance if you are vegetarian, as they don't always have a set meatless option.

Tapas Ole   8 Eyre Place   556 2754

Quite the contrary here, the atmosphere is bright, lively and, well, Spanish. For those not familiar with the concept of tapas, it is a style of eating whereby there are a number of different, smaller dishes, which are picked at by as many as want to share. This started, apparently, with Spanish bartenders covering their clients glasses with saucers ('tapas') to keep out flies. This evolved into placing some olives or nuts on the plate to 'tapar el apetito' (put a lid on the appetite). Soon there are cheeses and chorizo being offered also and tapas is born! Tapas Ole does a much broader range now, with meats and fish the staples, and a few veggie options too. Tapas has become quite popular these days in Edinburgh, with even a few pubs taking the type on board, but this is the real home of the genre, so to speak.

Rick's   55a Frederick Street   622 7800

I had originally intended to include Rick's in the Drinking section of the guide, but then I had a meal there recently and realised I absolutely had to move it here, since it is one of the best restaurants in Edinburgh. The modern wooden décor is still intimate thanks to the candlelight and the dining room at the back seems to have been built on a veranda, with a glass ceiling allowing you to look straight up the stone wall above. The menu is excellent and it took my wife and I an age to choose from the offered options, particularly impressive when you know she's vegetarian and couldn't make her mind up. When the food came it so far exceeded our expectations of a bar/restaurant's capabilities that we had to actually admit to the manager our surprise, only to discover they have an award-winning chef in the kitchen, as well as an award-winning barman serving cocktails. Far better than just an upmarket cocktail bar, and I humbly apologise for misjudging it initially. I particularly recommend the scallops in hazelnut butter.

Victoria & Albert   15-17 Frederick Street   226 4562

I got the shock of my life when I discovered this place recently. It used to be a fairly traditional style pub, but now it's gone all glass and manners! Very nice it is too, as I can testify having only made it there for lunch at the weekend. The glass top tables are a bit odd, I'm not used to seeing my legs as I eat, if you know what I mean, but still stylish. The menu is a good one though, with excellent presentation, especially of the soups! Worth a lunchtime bite if you want better than just a pub meal.

Hard Rock Café   18-20 George Street   260 3000

Well, as I've said many times before, if you haven't heard of the Hard Rock Café, then you haven't been paying attention! For those who haven't, there are actually three businesses at work here: 1. Restaurant serving American/Chargrill style food in mammoth (no, really) portions, with lots of music memorabilia and rock videos on the wall. Service is very good and friendly. This was the last place I saw the video for Pearl Jam's 'Jeremy' and I have fond memories of it, even just for that. 2. Cocktail bar serving anything you can imagine, and some stuff you wouldn't. Bonus is you can get any of them at your table with your meal too! 3. Shop, selling all kinds of branded clothing etc for the HRC. Good fun, more of an event than a dinner, and worth taking a large group along to for a fun night out.

Le Chambertin George Hotel, 19-21 George Street   225 1251

Hotel Restaurants can be hit and miss – not so with Le Chambertin. Fully deserving of it's status as one of Edinburgh's outstanding venues, if you happen to be staying here, you must eat in the hotel at least once! If you're staying elsewhere, don't worry: all welcome. The food is very Scottish, not only in ingredients but also in design, so again, you'll get a genuine taste of the local diet. Well, actually, you'll probably be eating better than most of us!

The Dome   14 George Street   624 8624

Set in a former bank building, the main feature of this bar/restaurant is, well, the dome, predictably. To be fair, though, it might not be The Duomo, but it's pretty impressive. The food is mostly chargrill style; burgers, fish and the like, and with the name of the restaurant being 'The Grill Room', that's no real surprise. Nice setting for a decent meal, basically.

La Lanterna   83 Hanover Street   226 3090

I know this will sound a bit 'Disney', but when you eat here, you're not so much a customer as a guest. The place is always full of regulars, which can't be a bad sign, and Toni and Tony Zaino, who have been running this little Italian for many years now, welcome them with open arms and big smiles. And, if you happen to have written a nice review about them, they might even pretend to pour a glass of wine on your head. Food wise, it is simple but well done. This is not a pizza place, but the pasta is fresh and I particularly recommend the steak with a brandy cream sauce. In fact, I may go there for dinner this weekend, now that I'm thinking about it...

Nargile   73 Hanover Street   225 5755

Nargile was well established as an Aberdeen favourite before Seyhan Azak brought this excellent Turkish restaurant to Edinburgh recently. Frankly, the food here is wonderful, with mezze (a Turkish kind of tapas) to start followed by an absolutely mouth-watering array of

TRADITIONAL FISH & CHIPS - WINES - SPIRITS - ICE CREAM
AUTHENTIC ITALIAN PIZZAS - PASTAS - PANINI - CAFFÈ

L'ALBA D'ORO

Established 1975

OPENING HOURS:
Monday - Friday Lunchtime: 11.30am - 1.30pm
Monday - Sunday Evenings: 5pm - 12am

5-11 Henderson Row, Edinburgh, EH3 5DH - Tel/Fax: 0131 557 2580

mains, including all kinds of barbecued and grilled meats, vegetables and pitta bread. If you want my advice, and if you're reading this you probably do, you absolutely have to try the haloumi, the stuffed vine leaves and the filo stuffed with feta from the mezze options and the traditional baklava for dessert. As for a main course, well, if there's not something here that excites you, you're probably already dead. There's also Turkish beer, Efes, which is worth a sip. Oh, just try everything, trust me…

Siam Erawan   48 Howe Street   226 3675

The Erawan family has been another pleasant introduction to Edinburgh. There are three in total, all in the New Town and all offer good high quality Oriental cuisine, especially satays and vegetable dishes, with banquet options also on offer. Siam is probably the classiest of the three, with candlelit archways to eat under for a cosy meal for two. The other two come later, one quite soon…

Erawan Express   176 Rose Street   220 0059

I presume the name follows on from Supermarkets who branded themselves as 'Express' or 'Metro' when what they meant was small and convenient. There's certainly no rush in the smallest Erawan, but it's more compact and designed for people in a hurry for lunch so they can get back to work.

Mussel Inn   61-65 Rose Street   225 5979

Believe it or not, this is a seafood restaurant specialising in: mussels! Oh and scallops and oysters, too. There's also a smattering of other fish on offer and the catch of the day changes daily, but these are the three basic staples. You know they're going to be decent, since the restaurant themselves have a farm on which they grow the main ingredients. It is quite a casual little place and perfect for a less formal meal, if a touch pricey. Apparently, it is a big favourite of Clarissa Dickson-Wright, who manages to merit her second mention in this guide so far…

The Bad Ass Café & Bistro   167 Rose Street   225 1546

Before we go on to anything else – isn't that a great name for a bistro bar? You really expect to find John Shaft in the bar having a cocktail with a bevy of scantily clad beauties, don't you? Failing that, you can just stop in for a bite to eat, of course. Having had major cosmetic surgery in the last two years, The Bad Ass has gone from being a pub named after an evil donkey, to a very nice little West End eatery. Describing themselves as serving 'Fine wine, ales and ketchup' (presumably all by the glass) they do a decent turn in whisky haggis and chargrill, with separate lunch and evening menus. A nice mid-range place for a bite, if that's what you're in the mood for. At this rate, they'll give that donkey a good name…

Yo Sushi   66 Rose Street   220 6040

If Oloroso is London come to Edinburgh, then I suppose this is Tokyo doing the same. To my knowledge this is the first proper sushi bar in Edinburgh, conveyor belt and all, so you get the sport of trying to catch your food before you eat it. It's safe to say, you either like sushi or you don't, but if you do – here it is, modern Japanese styling and all.

Erawan Oriental   14 South St Andrew Street   556 4242

The biggest of the three is, well, the biggest. Large and airy, it offers more seating and therefore gets even busier than the other two. It is also located just off Princes Street, so is convenient if you don't really know the town well or are shopping for the day and in need of some lunch.

Bell's Diner   7 St Stephen Street   225 8116

This is a wee American inspired place with no pretensions, but it has two things going for it that make it very recommendable: great burgers and great milkshakes. Trust me, you don't need to know anything else.

Blue Parrot Cantina   49 St Stephen Street   225 2941

A rustic basement Mexican with the unusual delight of an outdoor toilet(!), this is another in the growing number of good Mexicans in town. The ruddy brown walls and wooden furniture give it an air of authenticity and they have some good stuff on the menu. Among the unusual things are deep fried jalapenos stuffed with cream cheese, strawberry margaritas (you knew I'd mention the margaritas) and sweet chimichangas filled with fruit. The parrot has absolutely no significance, other than that this premises has been called that for as long as anyone can remember.

Ping On   26 Deanhaugh Street   332 3621

A long standing resident of Stockbridge, well, since 1969 anyway, which is pretty damn good for a restaurant, Ping On is a good solid bet for a nice meal out. Cantonese, Szechwan and Peking are on offer. This is another that is well liked by locals, which is a sign that they're doing it well and consistently.

Pizza Express   1 Deanhaugh Street   332 7229

Same fare and standard as the other Pizza Express, this has the added advantage of being in a great building, which overlooks the Water of Leith and Stockbridge itself. On a sunny day it's glorious to sit at the windows in the back room with the river running underneath.

The Buffalo Grill   1 Raeburn Place   332 3864

Another that's popular with Edinburghers, this second branch of the Buffalo Grill opened in 1999. With a selection of 10 different ways to have your steak and 7 different burgers, you can guess what the speciality is! There's also a range of fish and chicken dishes and an imaginative, if smaller selection of vegetarian dishes too, so everyone can eat, not just the steak lovers. They are happy for you to bring in your own bottle or to select from their own small wine list.

The Stockbridge Restaurant 54 St Stephen Street   226 6766

Brand new in town, this is the restaurant everyone's talking about right now. In a little basement on St Stephen Street, a little haven of peace, style and good food has evolved. The menu and the wine list are not extensive, but the seasonal offer is cooked fresh and extremely well. Impressive fireplace and decadent black stone walls – very much worth a trip to Stockbridge on its own. Little touches like the sorbets offered between courses to cleanse the palate justify the upmarket cost, but by the time you get the bill, you won't care anyway.

Le Café St Honore
34 Thistle Street Lane North West   226 2211

Probably the best French restaurant in Edinburgh, Café St Honore has won barrel loads of praise from all kinds of guides and associations, including celebrated British critic AA Gill. The décor is French and intimate and the cuisine is classic – exactly what you'd expect from a little Parisian gem. And, of course, there's the location – the address is so long because it's not easy to find, tucked away just off Thistle Street, which is no main thoroughfare itself. But this just lends it an air of je ne sais quoi that makes it that much more of a treasure to find.

Caffe D.O.C.
49a Thistle Street   220 6846

Since D.O.C. stands for "Denominazione d'Origine Controllata", the Italian standard for wines of a certain quality and source, it's not surprising this is an authentic, high quality Italian itself. The food is also full-bodied and very pleasant on the nose, with an elite selection providing some unique yet very much appreciable flavours. Again, not so much pasta, more meat and fish here, showing that in Italy, pizza and pasta are not the only thing on the menu. Obviously, the wine is also very good – they couldn't really get away without that, now could they? – and you can sip it in the front bar while you wait for your table should you wish to. Don't be fooled by what you can see in the window, the body of the restaurant is at the back, next to the kitchen – something I always find comforting as it shows a degree of honesty and confidence in their preparation. Of course, it also gets the taste buds going when you smell the aromas drifting out to taunt you.

Fisher's in the City
58 Thistle Street   225 5109

The king of the seafood restaurants. Opened in 2001, this is the big brother of Fisher's, which has long been delighting the populace of Leith with its fresh seafood delicacies. There is a wide range of fish and shellfish on offer, served up in imaginative ways. The décor is dark wood with various nautical memorabilia lying around, more "South Pacific" than "Jules Verne" and there's also an excellent wine list, highly recommended by a wine-quaffing colleague of mine. Rapidly becoming one of the "places to be seen" in Edinburgh, it's another gem on this high quality lane.

WEST END AND LOTHIAN ROAD

Old Orleans
Fountain Park   228 8339

As opposed to New Orleans, obviously, except it's not French food you'll find here, but traditional Cajun stuff. This is a big open plan restaurant at the top of the Fountain Park building, with a little cocktail bar too. It's very family friendly and also attracts office nights out.

Food wise, if you don't know Cajun, it's spicy and includes things like Blackened Cajun Chicken and Jambalaya, which, frankly, taste as good as they sound. Another of my own favourites, but it's not particularly veggie friendly. Good place to stop in for a meal before taking the family to the cinema next door.

Blue Bar Café
10 Cambridge Street   221 1222

Set above the new (relatively) Traverse Theatre, Blue is a stylish and modern bar café that attracts theatregoers, local workers and just plain Edinburghers. The décor is all light wood and metal and there's plenty of natural light coming in.

Food wise it's basically your standards done in new and exciting ways, with Blue's trademark sausages being the perfect example, with pork, veal and lemon or Mediterranean beef and some exotic delicacies thrown in for good measure. This place was actually recommended to me by a friend who absolutely insisted I try the Malteser ice cream, which I haven't managed yet, but if it tastes as good as he described…well!

Lazio Restaurant
95 Lothian Road   229 7788

Thee are quite a few Italians in the West End, but this is my own favourite. Opened in 1981, it is now run by the second generation of the Crolla family. The décor is modern and smart, while the staff are extremely friendly and helpful – all "career waiters and chefs". The menu is much as you'd expect from an Italian, with pizzas and pastas the mainstay. If you're looking for that kind of meal, this is as good an option as we have. Be sure to book though – the last time my wife and I tried to drop in for a table on a Friday night, we couldn't get in the door!

Old Orleans
30 Grindlay Street   229 1511

While the Old Orleans in Fountain Park is brand new, this one has been around for at least 15 years or so. It's the same Cajun menu, with a separate cocktail bar and attracts the Theatregoers and workers in the area as well as those just out for a nice meal. This one is more suited to couples and grown ups, being a bit darker and more intimate, where the other is more family friendly - in my experience anyway.

Stac Polly · 8a Grindlay Street · 229 5405

Another location for the very Scottish, Stac Polly restaurant, also serving the best in Scottish cuisine. See the New Town write up for more information.

The Atrium · 10 Cambridge Street · 228 8882

Another restaurant fanatic recently recommended this restaurant to me and I was appalled at not having been before when she described it to me. I immediately tried to book a table for that evening, only to discover it was booked solid that night and the next, which tells you how popular it is.

This gem of a restaurant, located, like Blue, in the same building as the Traverse Theatre, was opened in 1993 by chef Andrew Radford, who went on to win The Macallan Personality of the Year in 1994. The restaurant itself is intimate and subtly lit, while the food is the best in fine dining, with options like breast of Gressingham duck, bok choi, sticky belly pork, lentil and coriander sauce or seared rare tuna with cannellini bean salad and red wine jus. One of the more expensive options in Edinburgh, but also one of the top candidates for best restaurant. Be sure to book!

The Great Wall · 105-109 Lothian Road · 229 7595

There's an old adage that if you ever want to know whether to drink the Guinness in a Dublin pub, check if the locals are drinking it first. This equally applies to international restaurants and so it is a high recommendation that a large number of Oriental customers are often found in The Great Wall. The restaurant is actually huge, doing justice to its name, and has one main large room with many circular tables dotted throughout it, with several little anterooms. In fact, it is slightly reminiscent of a hotel ballroom filled with diners. That said, I understand that this is a cultural thing in the Orient and makes it all the more authentic.

The Marque Central · Royal Lyceum, 30b Grindlay Street · 229 9859

Attached to The Lyceum, like all the restaurants up here this attracts a pre-theatre crowd, for convenience if nothing else. The else that goes with it is the elegant, modern and artistic atmosphere in which to dine before expanding your cultural horizons at any of the three theatrical venues within minutes' walking distance. The Marque Central is the second of its type in the city, the first being out on Causewayside, and the formula they have works – striking atmosphere, good food and friendly efficient service. Just right to get you in the mood for a bit of Shakespeare or Big Band.

Rogue · 67 Morrison Street · 228 2700

Part of the major office building that Scottish Widows have here, my lovely wife took me here for a birthday night out last year and what a great present it was. Rogue is extremely modern in design, with an almost Oriental touch to it. There are two distinct sections: an elegant and relaxing cocktail lounge with some excellent margaritas, and a large, sprawling white cloth dining room, again with the Oriental feel, probably because of the dark wood decorating all the walls, while the rest of the décor is very clean and light.

The service here is absolutely excellent; not surprising since proprietor Dave Ramsden is often found out on the floor supervising the staff and serving tables personally. The food is also excellent, with a nouvelle cuisine basis. My abiding memory of our meal though was an excellent bottle of wine, which we never even noticed the waiter continually topping up our glasses with, and the dessert: a rich chocolate mousse topped with handmade orange sorbet – the two tastes were dramatically different but complemented each other brilliantly. Rogue is now a firm favourite with us and we go whenever we have an excuse to.

Indian Cavalry Club · 3 Atholl Place · 228 3282

In my experience, there are arguably two restaurants vying for best Indian in Edinburgh, and this is one of them. The décor here is colonial India personified, right down to the regimental uniforms worn by the staff and the plants and screens dotted around the room to give the impression of the subcontinent. They even have an Officer's Mess, which actually gives the impression you are inside a massive tent, for special parties.

As for the food, I cannot begin to complain. It is, as I have said to many people, an experience that teaches you how Indian food is supposed to be prepared, right down to the homemade kulfi, which is much better than the pre-made version I have had elsewhere. It attracts a lot of business lunches and dinners due to the very formal atmosphere, but is also good for a dinner for two, or impressing the relatives, as we did with the father in law, who was again suitably impressed, being not a bad Indian cook in his own right. I understand tourist agencies from all over the world, including India and New York, call in advance to book in travelling parties, so that must be something of a recommendation. Another personal favourite.

Bar Roma · 39a Queensferry Street · 226 2977

Used to have lunch here often when my wife's office was nearby. This is another very large, open restaurant, with, for some reason, a tree growing right in the middle of it. It is fun and laid back, attracting, again, a lot of local businesses for lunches and all sorts for dinners. It's a good one for big nights out, as they have no problem with noisy or party here.

The menu is huge and has all kinds of standard Italian variations – the meatball dish I had on my last visit was great and actually too filling to finish. It's not about to win any culinary awards, but it is laid back and enjoyable, with pretty quick service of decent food, albeit a bit "cheeky chappie".

Bouzy Rouge   1a Alva Street   225 9594

You descend into this little underground restaurant and enter into something of another world. The place is like a little labyrinth, with bright colours complementing stone walls and a special 'garden' for larger parties to eat in. Bouzy is actually a little town in France, famous for its red wine, thus the name. Of course, that in mind, the wine menu is pretty good.

Food wise they've come up with quite a fusion menu, called "casual gourmet", which combines your everyday ingredients with the more exotic, meaning you can eat haggis and mashed potato (done with some imagination), while your partner tucks into a mushroom filo basket. Very enjoyable; good service and a unique little atmosphere make this worth trying.

Lafayette   9 Randolph Place   225 8678

Right. It's got a French name. It's in a mock Tudor style house with timber framing. And it's in Scotland's capital. So what kind of food and atmosphere should we expect here? Well, how about top Scottish ingredients cooked in a French style?

The food in this new restaurant is as elegant and cultured as the décor, which has everything down to the fleur-de-lys to make it special. Serving the likes of pumpkin soup with cinnamon ravioli and pan-fried Aberdeen Angus fillets in a red wine and shallot jus, with a large wine list, this is somewhere to come for a special meal, with a special person.

Pizza Express   32 Queensferry Street   225 8863

Couldn't say why really, but I've always thought this was the Pizza Express that did the best pizzas of the three – probably just my imagination. Anyway, this is much the same as the others, with front and back sections both having glass walls for lots of natural light. Don't be fooled by the seats at the back though, they're Indigo Yard's, not for eating pizza at! (See earlier Pizza Expresses in Stockbridge and the Bridges)

SOUTHSIDE, TOLLCROSS AND MORNINGSIDE

Buffalo Grill   12-14 Chapel Street   667 7427

The Buffalo Grill has been serving Edinburgh the best in steaks at affordable prices since 1986, and has been so successful as to have recently spawned a little brother down in the heart of fashionable Stockbridge. If you're partial to a side of beef, with all varieties of sauces and some chips (fries) on the side, this is the place for you, but don't shy away just because there's a veggie in your party! The owners recognised the need to have veggie options on their menu for just such an occasion and I believe there are usually at least three veggie meals to choose from, too. They have no license, but welcome you bringing in your own wine.

La Bonne Vie   49 Causewayside   667 1110

Known as a fresh young and affordable place for lunch or dinner, La Bonne Vie has a loyal following among the students and locals in the area. Its silver exterior is hard to miss and the natural wood and stone interior make for a comfortable and unpretentious atmosphere. Food wise it is Scottish fare with a twist of French style, as with many of Edinburgh's eateries (thank the Auld Alliance for that one!). Good quality and very reasonable (£5.00 for lunch).

The Marque   19 Causewayside   466 6660

A nice light restaurant that provides the same quality as its offshoot on Lothian Road, but with perhaps even a little more creativity in the dishes on offer. Cumin in the batter and salsa in the sweet potatoes are just some of the imaginative uses of seasoning on offer here, and the menu changes every fortnight, so you can always find a different dish with each visit. The restaurant itself is actually made up of three old antique shops and as such, the layout has some character to make your dining all the more interesting.

The New Bell   233 Causewayside   668 2868

The 'New' in the name would suggest a modern atmosphere, but in fact the New Bell has a very old world antique feel about it, not surprising with the number of antique stores up this way. Carved wooden chairs and old style paintings give it a real sense of history, even though the restaurant itself is only a few years old. It sits above The Old Bell pub, which does indeed have a bit of history about it, but the upstairs restaurant deserves just as many plaudits as its more well-established downstairs neighbour.

The menu has good traditional Scottish ingredients, again, but with a twist of the Mediterranean and Asian about them.

Wat's Chinese   44 Ratcliffe Terrace   668 1878

This is one of the less celebrated Chinese restaurants in Edinburgh, but word of mouth about it is very good. In fact, my mum pretty much has a standing weekly reservation here. That's because the staff are friendly, the décor is lovely and inviting (with the overhead mesh of fairy lights that went up a few years ago still there thanks to their popularity with the regulars) and the food is excellent.

If you should like to, they're also happy for you to bring in your own bottle of wine, for a small corkage charge, although they do have their own wine list too.

Ayutthaya   14b Nicolson Street   556 9351

One half of a Thai duet in Edinburgh, alongside Sukhothai, this is a nice variation on standard Oriental restaurants. Much like Chinese, except with a few twists: the prawn crackers have cumin through them and the meals favour hot and sweet combinations, like chilli plum sauces, for example. If you like Thai, this is a fine place to get it. The restaurant itself is intimate thanks to the lack of windows, and you'll feel quite hidden away from the world, which can be good if that's what you're looking for. They have a good vegetarian range and, being opposite the Festival theatre, pre-theatre dinners are not at all uncommon.

Dragon Way   74-78 South Clerk Street   668 1328

A very good and well-respected Chinese restaurant, the décor in here is as impressive as the food. There's a little pool of exotic fish in the middle of the room, for starters! This is more 'elegant', I suppose than many Chinese Restaurants and my mother-in-law has a particular fondness for it. Especially after she accidentally tried the prawn crackers and was enjoying them until someone pointed out that they were in fact made from prawns. This disturbed her somewhat, her having been vegetarian for about 20 years! We all laughed though…

Elephants & Bagels   37 Marshall Street   668 4404

What a bizarre combination, I'm sure you're thinking. What would an elephant and a bagel have in common? A mortal fear of mice, maybe? Well, there is an explanation. You see, this is a spin off of the extremely successful Elephant House (mentioned in the Old Town section) and they specialise in…bagels! Thus…

I have never actually managed to get in here, but I recommend it anyway, because I have TRIED to get in for lunch on several occasions, but the place is so damn popular at lunchtime that it's always heaving and I never had time to wait! I have, however spoken to several people who have told me it is great and that their selection of sweet and savoury bagels with a variety of fillings are a joy. Just try not to go right in the middle of the working lunch hour (Monday to Friday, 12-2) as you'll struggle for a table!

Kalpna   2-3 St Patrick's Square   667 9890

A fantastic and original restaurant, this is a strictly vegetarian Indian. I was entirely unsure about this, but as my wife is veggie and loves Indian food I was happy to go along and check it out. As it happened, I absolutely loved it and we've been back several times since. They do things you would never imagine would work, and yet they are wonderful: paneer (Indian cheese) in a tomato and honey sauce, or lentils in a garlic based sauce for example. They also do wonderful desserts, like gulabjamon in syrup. (If you don't know what that is, trust me, you want to know)

Décor wise, I notice they've had a relatively recent makeover, going from the more traditional Indian décor to a quite modern and elegant white look. Prices are not at all unreasonable. One small hint, if you're booking in advance, ask for a table in the back, as it's a bit more private away from the windows and the street.

Nicolson's Restaurant   6a Nicolson Street   557 4567

This was always considered quite a 'cool' place to hang out for the afternoon, meet friends or just have a coffee or herbal tea and chill out. The wide-open spaces up on this first floor eatery along with the deep bold colours give it a very distinct personality and it attracts all walks of life.

Since it was revealed as the legendary writing place of adopted Scot and Harry Potter creator JK Rowling though, it has become much more famous and is more than likely featured on a few of Edinburgh's tours by now. So if you want to try your hand at some literary inspiration or just want to see where the adventures of the little wizard sprang from, look no further.

The Vine Leaf   22a Nicolson Street   662 9191

This is a lovely little underground restaurant with a Mediterranean menu that has all the right ingredients to be a success. The owner is a lovely Egyptian (I think!) woman, who started out by letting a load of her friends tell her which of her dishes should be on the menu. Then she set out to provide a comfortable and homely atmosphere for people to relax in and then she hired some of the friendliest and chattiest staff I've ever had the pleasure to be served by. Another that is very reasonably priced and quite casual. I like to go in for lunch whenever I'm in the area. Just for the record, it only used to be an Italian, so don't go in and ask for pizza – they don't do it!

The Wok Bar   26-30 Potter Row   667 8594

I've never been quite sure whether this is a bar that serves food or a restaurant that has a bar. I think the lines have blurred so much these days that it hardly matters anymore anyway. I know it best for food, though, having been in once or twice for a bite of its Thai and Chinese fare, which is served up in generous portions, although when I was last there the veggie options were limited. They did say, however, that they were looking into that, so…

The décor is extremely modern and stylish – there's really not much of the traditional Orient about it and it's more, to my mind, like a London Sushi bar or some such.

Fenwick's   15 Salisbury Place   667 4265

Tucked away just on the edge of the commercial part of the Southside, but nicely on the end of a quiet little residential street is an intimate and relaxing restaurant serving well-cooked local produce. A light wooden and unfussy décor is just perfect for the surrounds and whether you're looking for somewhere to go with a large group or dinner for two, this is a good option. If you're staying down this end of town, it is arguably the best restaurant nearby and it is not at all bad for price. They also serve breakfast on a Sunday until 6 o'clock, which can't be a bad thing if you've been out for few on Saturday night!

Blonde Restaurant   75 St Leonards Street   668 2917

Now, if memory serves me right, this was once a Howie's, but the chef decided to take it over and converted it into Blonde. Whether or not he is blonde, loves Debbie Harry or is just fond of Belgian beers is beyond me. It matters not.

What does matter is that this is a nice relaxed casual atmosphere to have a good quality inexpensive meal in. The interior decor is very IKEA in look, if a bit better in quality (don't tell the Swedes I said that!) and the menu has the same laid back feel, with a fairly international spread of dishes. This is another one my mum is quite fond of, and I'm suddenly noticing that all the restaurants she likes are within ten minutes of her house. Hmmm…

Mother's   107 St Leonard's Street   662 0772

Apart from the vivid orange exterior, there's not much about this place, on the face of it, to suggest that it is in fact a rather good Mexican. So, you'll just have to take my word for it! Two rooms inside have the customary dark wooden furniture which seems to be required before you will be granted a license to serve Mexican food anywhere in the city!

Food-wise they have most of the standards plus a few special extras that will appear on the big chalkboard up on the wall, like fish that is in-season and the like. They do a particularly good thing that I cannot for the life of me remember the name of, which is basically two large round crispy fried tortillas full of spicy meat, beans and cheese. This is, I believe, my sister's favourite Mexican in town…

Phenecia   55-57 West Nicolson Street   662 4493

This is a very casual and friendly little North African and Mediterranean restaurant that is popular with local students, professors and other people from all over the city who have been lucky enough to discover it! I was introduced for the first time to tapas here and every time I go back I find it difficult not to simply have the bnadek (spicy lamb meatballs in a tangy sauce) and the steak fillets in a savoury lemon sauce, so much do I enjoy them. It's definitely the sauces that are so addictive, but the meat they complement is cooked to perfection and melts in your mouth. There are lots of veggie options too and, basically, I'd be surprised if there's not something here to satisfy everyone. And the prices, especially for lunch, are extremely reasonable.

Pig's Bistro   41 West Nicolson Street   667 6676

Another casual little place (they're common up here!), Pigs is quite small (seats about 20 or so). The food is varied and comes from all different regions, with them usually having a spread of something like Chinese, Italian, French and British options on the go. The menu goes up on the chalkboard daily. I had a particularly excellent Italian pasta and meatball dish here once and have remembered it fondly for ever after. I also came here for lunch with my mum on my last day in a job

I desperately wanted out of and went back after lunch more than a little intoxicated by the great bottle of wine she brought with her (they're happy for you to bring in your own!), so the rest of the afternoon involved accomplishing very little and laughing a lot!

Susie's Wholefood Diner
51-53 West Nicolson Street   667 8729

This is where many of Edinburgh's health conscious and particularly vegetarian come to eat. The format is not at all fussy, you grab a tray and queue for what you want, and take your pick of the healthy meal of the day. There are pulses and leaves galore to be had here, and what they do with them can be rather tasty. It's not the kind of thing I'd want to eat every day, but if that's your kind of diet, this is one of the best places to fill up. I think they also cater for vegans, but don't quote me on that; it's not my speciality subject.

Ndebele   57 Home Street   221 1141

Opened in 1996, this claims to be the only Southern African restaurant in Scotland and, in lieu of visiting every town in Scotland to make sure, I'm prepared to believe that. This is another place that I heard about by word of mouth and I always consider that a good thing. They not only serve South African food, but offer artefacts, cards and jewellery too. It's a very casual atmosphere and they offer takeaway as well as sit in meals. For those in the know, they sell boerewors (a special sausage with coriander) and cornbread (a favourite of my own!). Even if it's just for novelty value, you should pop in here if you can.

Shamiana   14 Brougham Street   228 2265

This is the other restaurant that can rightly claim to be the best Indian restaurant in Edinburgh. So much so, in fact, that it also has a claim on Scotland, with Patak's having voted it best Indian Restaurant in Scotland in 1995 and the 1998 Good Curry Guide awarding their chef, Pat Chapman, the best chef in Britain! It's hard to argue with awards like that and my 50 something year old Publisher tells me that he has long loved it, so it seems that ever since it opened in 1977 it has been reaching such culinary heights – so much so that he is prepared to drive from Leith to pick up a takeaway when there are others nearer and prepared to deliver.

The décor is not so grand and opulent as its competitor, the Cavalry Club, but it is more than pleasant and prides itself more on the quality of it's food anyway, and rightly so. The dishes on offer are from North India and Kashmir, for those who know their stuff, and they offer a special deal on Tuesday nights for 3 courses and a bottle of Cobra beer of just £12.95.

Sukhothai   23 Brougham Street   229 1537

The sister Thai restaurant to Ayutthaya, Sukhothai is more open and traditionally laid out, with plenty of light coming in. The menu is much the same with the standard Thai influences like coconut milk and plum sauces. Was here for a work night out once upon a time and we all had a great feed and also managed to get very drunk To their eternal credit, the staff put up with us with good humour all night, even up until we were the last to be thrown out of the place so they could finally close. Marvellous.

Montpelier's   159-161 Bruntsfield Place   229 3115

Open all day, Montpelier's is an upmarket bar/bistro that serves breakfast, lunch or dinner in a choice of two areas, or three if you can sit outside in the sun at the time. The menu has an international feel, with things like teriyaki tuna steak and poached salmon on the menu. It has a very loyal following in the area and definitely lives up to its "special" billing.

There are many ways to judge the success of Montpelier's. You could consider that it has survived for many years as a well-respected eatery in a part of town where the locals are notoriously selective about where they will or won't go. You could also think about the fact that from this one venue, a company that has produced such Edinburgh luminaries as Indigo Yard, Rick's, Favorit and the new Opal Lounge has sprung. Or you could just go in and try the fare and see for yourself why it has earned the reputation that it has.

Parrots   3 Viewforth   229 3252

Parrots is fun. The menu is hand written and is so extensive that it requires a table of contents. The options are wide-ranging and include sections of pre-starters, starters, meat dishes (British, European and Spicy sections), vegetarian options (an impressive 10 main courses), seafood and side dishes. Then there are desserts which are broken down into cold, hot and "Macaws", which are various concoctions of muffin, ice-cream, liquers, cream and anything else they decide to throw in. The atmosphere is friendly and relaxed and the service is too, including an attempt to hurry if you need them to and help to select dishes suitable to a special diet.

And then there's the parrots themselves, which form a large part of the décor. Well, they would, wouldn't they? Finally, a restaurant that promises an animal and actually delivers! (Sort of…)

The Apartment   7-13 Barclay Place   228 6456

The Apartment opened amid a fair bit of excitement a year or two ago and it was on everyone's lips. It actually has a fairly simple formula clean, uncluttered and smart décor with a relaxed edge and some artwork to feast your eyes on, with a slightly unusual (options like "Chunky Healthy") menu of Mediterranean and International influences. They don't seem to advertise much and that has given them something of a mystique that has helped the buzz to remain throughout, with the restaurant regularly booked out and queues for seats. The jovial and friendly staff don't hurt either. If you fancy trying this out, book in advance by at least a few days if you want to have any hope of a table, especially at the weekend.

EAST END AND PORTOBELLO

Ferri's   1 Antigua Street   556 5592

I mention Ferri's for a very specific reason. It has a good general reputation and its small size makes it possible for the affable Italian waiters to give everyone good, personal service. I have only been here a few times, and always for their pizzas, which are very good. The one thing they have that not everyone else has is a tendency to stay open late, which helps if you have been out for a few drinks and fancy a sit down meal en route home.

A friend and I, a few years back, came in here a few beers past sober at about midnight and made an attempt to order a pepperoni pizza to share. Unfortunately, my friend's "Can you do a pepperoni pizza?" came out as "Due pepperoni pizzas" to the waiter, which he translated as "Two pepper pizzas". Much hilarity ensued as we tried to explain when they arrived that we had wanted one pepperoni ("No, no, not peppers, spicy sausage, yeah?") pizza and not the two we had been presented with. It all came good in the end though and we were not thrown out for giggling at the mix up. Thus, I consider them very nice people and always have.

Giuliano's   18-19 Union Place   556 6590

Friendly and lively Italian that is very popular with group nights out and families. At Christmas time they are absolutely packed with Festive revellers and the whole place just has a permanent fun atmosphere about it. The Italian options are unsurprising and the prices perfectly fair – it's mostly the relaxed party vibe that makes this a stand out. Being just opposite the Playhouse doesn't hurt either, with pre and post theatre parties always welcome.

Prince Balti House   11-12 Seafield Road East   657 1155

Portobello has never been famous for great restaurants (to my knowledge anyway), but this new arrival may be about to set a new trend. Prince Balti is the newest effort from the same stall as Britannia Spice and with those kind of credentials, it will be interesting to see how it develops, and if it can draw the custom out to Portobello to sample their broad range of subcontinent fare. If it wins half the awards its big brother has, it'll be a resounding success!

Howie's   29 Waterloo Place   556 5766

This Howie's may well have the grandest setting of all. Their formula of unfussy fine dining is served up in a wonderful old Georgian building off the East end of Princes Street, with absolutely amazing views of Arthur's Seat out of the huge bay windows. If surroundings are important to your dining experience, this is not one to miss and it is very convenient for the city centre without being smack dab in the middle of town, so it's relatively quiet.

LEITH

Skipper's Bistro   1a Dock Place   554 1018

In a historic port like Leith you'd expect to see quite a few seafood restaurants and you'd be quite right – there are several good ones. Skipper's Bistro has been attracting custom to Leith for over twenty years now, preceding the upgrading of Leith from port to fashionable restaurant location by a good ten years. These days it has some competition but those who know it still soundly laud it.

Slightly hidden away in a lovely old building, it does suffer slightly for being hard to find – but it is very much worth the effort. There's a selection of starters, soups, mussels, oysters or prawns to begin, followed by around 8 various fish dishes and a meat dish. Again, it's not cheap, but it is good and worth the money you pay.

The Rock   78 Commercial Street   555 2225

An extremely elegant and stylish restaurant that prides itself on one thing in particular: its steaks. This is not a veggie friendly place, but they do know several different ways to make a steak fantastic. They also know how to make your dining an experience, by letting you see the chef in action and giving good service in a very upmarket setting.

Again, the prices reflect the quality, and the Rock also suffers a little from the same disease as its neighbours – not enough people know about the number of great places down here, so they're not getting much "passing trade". Trust me – make the effort – you'll be pleased you did.

Waterfront Wine Bar   1c Dock Place   554 7427

As the name suggests, this lovely little red brick building houses a great little wine bar that sits right on the Water of Leith. The original building used to be the administrative centre for all the casual dockers who would work on the boats and there are still accounting books lying around the place as evidence of this. The conservatory at the back was recently torn down and a new, even nicer one built in its place. You can also even sit on a lower little pontoon in the better weather should you want to.

Why do I mention a wine bar here? Because it is also a cracking restaurant, serving a daily changing menu which usually attracts your editor for lunch or an early evening dinner meeting at least once a week. The fare is mostly seafood, but there are always variants, including at least one veggie starter and one main course each day. And, of course, there are a ridiculous number of wines to choose from to accompany your meal.

Britannia Spice   150 Commercial Street   555 2255

This is a real fusion of British and Indian culture. The décor is absolutely immaculate, with mini sails and a polished wooden floor giving the effect of the Royal Yacht itself, inside a former whisky bond! The service is also extremely good and the waiting staff are all outfitted in something reminiscent of the colonial age of India. The menu offers

The very best Indian Restaurant located by Portobello Beach
The finest classic top restaurant in Edinburgh

THE PRINCE

Special offers

Take-away meal orders of **£40** or more will receive a **free bottle** of house wine.

Party of ten people or more receive a **free bottle** of Indian beer each with our compliments.

Gold Card Royalty members will receive a **25% discount** when sitting in.

A **15% discount** off any **special occasions** (birthdays, weddings) on parties over 20 people.

Balti House

BANGLADESHI & INDIAN CUISINE

FULLY LICENSED & FULLY AIR CONDITIONED

OPEN 7 DAYS

Lunch 12noon - 2pm
Dinner 5pm - 11.30pm
Friday - Saturday 5pm - 12am

FREE HOME DELIVERY SERVICE
(Minimum order £10)

We accept all normal credit cards:
Visa, mastercard, Switch etc

Special discounts

Special 20% discount for NHS staff and City of Edinburgh Council staff

Also for the staff and guests of the Balmoral Hotel, Carlton Hotel, Hotel Crown Plaza, McDonald Hotel, Hilton Hotel, Holiday Inn, Travel Inn and Kings' Manor Hotel

Highly Recommended

11/12 SEAFIELD ROAD EAST, EDINBURGH EH15 1EB

Tel: **0131 657 1155** or Fax: **0131 657 1122**

THE WATERFRONT
WINE BAR & BISTRO

One of the oldest, most established restaurants in Leith. Over-looking the dockside. Fine cuisine and wine available daily

1c Dock Place, Leith, Edinburh, EH6 6LU TEL: 0131 55407427 FAX: 0131 555 6060 www.sjf.co.uk

food from various regions of the subcontinent and is a more wide-ranging selection than many places usually bother to have. They also seem to have catered their fare to a more British palate, taking the sting out of some of their dishes and even offering some European standards, like steak and chips, to cater for those from the nearby hotel and also for any members of the family who may not be quite so adventurous.

Britannia Spice has won all kinds of awards and it is certainly worth a visit for a good meal in some unique and very special surroundings. If you want to introduce yourself to Indian food for the first time, this would be a good place to start.

Domenico's   30 Sandport Street   467 7266

A family run little Italian restaurant tucked away just off Commercial Street, Domenico's opened just three years ago. It's a friendly place with a good wine selection and the menu is a little bit different, with a range of pastas that deviate from your standard bolognaise and carbonara fare. For example, there are: chickpeas, blue cheese and roast peppers with tomato or bacon, peas and brie with cream and tomato pastas to be tried. There's also a daily selection of fresh meat produce and special pastas too. My colleague has a habit of eating here and getting exceptionally gruntled on the wine, which seems to make him a very valued customer!

Giuliano's on the Shore   1 Commercial Street   554 5272

Another Italian, this is more the standard pasta and pizza fare, but the main thing going for it is, it's extremely family friendly. Not only does it have a "fun" ethos about it, the kids can even see their pizzas being made while they wait. Perfect for a family meal out with the under 12's.

Gulnar's Passage to India
46 Queen Charlotte Street   554 7520

Another of my own favourite little restaurants in Edinburgh, Gulnar's is not only good food, but it's got a great layout too. As you go in, there's one level, which then has a split-level balcony going up and another lower level too. The whole place is then decorated in hanging sheets and the like and to top off the exotic feel, if you're very lucky, you might even get belly dancers at your table! A great fun night out or a nice intimate place for a romantic meal – either way this place is a gem. Oh and the food's great too, which is always a good thing…

Zinc Bar & Grill   Ocean Terminal   553 8070

The newest Conran Restaurant is the culinary jewel of Ocean Terminal and a fine jewel it is too. The grill style kitchen is open plan; the restaurant itself is huge, with metal décor and massive windows looking out over the water.
Food wise, the menu is very cosmopolitan, with a heavy grilled meats influence, but also having Macaroni Cheese alongside Vegetable Pad Thai. A good selection of wines and champagne is complemented by

any sort of beers or spirits you may want from the bar part of the business. And it's pretty good, too.

Fisher's Bistro   1 Shore   554 5666

This is the original that Fisher's in the City sprang up from. Long known in Leith as an excellent seafood restaurant, the fare here is as good as ever and, being in the heart of a seafood heaven, it shines like a little beacon all to itself. Well renowned far and wide for the quality of its fare. 'President' Blair, our beloved Prime Minister, was spotted dragging Mrs Blair from here in something of a hurry a few years back. I understand he 'forgot' to leave a tip!

(fitz)Henry   19 Shore Place   555 6625

We were lucky enough to be here for a meal recently on the occasion of the restaurant's first anniversary under the current owners, and a lovely evening we had. We began by being well entertained by the very jovial staff, who actually turned out to be the owners themselves. After being offered a glass of a highly recommended wine to decide if that was what we wanted, we were then served some delicious nibbles just to whet our appetites for the excellent meal that was to come.

This is a beautiful old stone building, formerly a warehouse, I believe, just off the Shore itself, and the décor has been done in a tastefully elegant style that gives quite an intimate gothic feel to it. The food is nouvelle cuisine in style with French, Mediterranean and Moroccan influences, but surprisingly filling, when often I find myself needing a snack on the way home after such fare. A lovely, if slightly more pricey venue for an intimate meal for two, or, as we did, a fun evening for four.

Malmaison   1 Tower Place   468 5000

Recently renovated to a very modern, geometric look, this is an excellent French style restaurant, which confirms the reputation it has around town. Actually a hotel, with both a bar and restaurant, Malmaison is associated very much with quality and prides itself on such. The building itself is quite a stand out right at the north end of the Shore, with its own little courtyard out front adding to the sense of grandeur about the place. Again, not cheap, but upmarket and considered well worth it.

Restaurant Martin Wishart   54 The Shore   553 3557

Before I had been here a few times, I was being regaled about including them in this guide: 'Oh, you must mention Martin Wishart – it's the only Edinburgh restaurant to have a Michelin star, you know!'. I haven't checked to confirm it is the only one, so don't take that as gospel. However I have checked out the restaurant and it is absolutely excellent.

There's only a small menu for lunch, with usually only two or three choices at most, but the evening menu is more extensive. Seafood is usually on the menu, along with game, pork, or chicken. Each meal I have had here has been absolutely without fault and I must make particular mention of the apple crumble I had some weeks ago now, which was far and away the best I've ever tried. There's also a good selection of wine. The restaurant itself is rather small, but well designed with clean, elegant lines and white décor giving it a 'special' atmosphere. I should also mention that Martin Wishart himself was short listed for this year's Drambuie Chef of the Year Award, the culinary Oscars. Must try if you're in the area. If you're not, make the effort anyway, but be sure to book first.

Shore Bar & Restaurant   3-4 Shore   555 0409

Continuing in the family vein, this is my Grandparents' favourite restaurant in Edinburgh and the one we went to for their Golden Anniversary lunch a few years ago. This is a character filled old wooden bar, with a separate white linen dining room and you can choose to eat in either. The menu changes all the time to accommodate the freshness of the food on offer, but again it is predominately seafood with some other options and usually at least one veggie. In the evening, you can also hang around after dinner for some live music, either Latin jazz or folk.

The Vintner's Rooms   The Vaults, 87 Giles Street   554 6767

Set just to the south of The Shore itself, The Vaults now hosts both this great restaurant and the Scotch Malt Whisky Society. The reason for the name is that the wine trade has long bee established in this building, firstly as a storage room and then as the headquarters of the Edinburgh Vintners Guild. You can choose to eat in two very different setting here: The white linen Auctioneers Alcove, which has 18th Century plasterwork by Thomas Clayton, or the Wine Bar, with the original old wine bins on display in a beautiful old wooden decor room. The food is French/Mediterranean in influence and there are 200 wines to choose from, as you'd expect in such a place. Another that is not inexpensive, but it has a great deal to make it worth the cost.

drinking & clubbing

Drinking and Scotland pretty much go hand in hand. And why wouldn't they? When we live in a country where the weather gets so cold we invented whisky just to warm ourselves up, you would expect a great deal of indoor activities to fill up the social calendar.

Socialising over a pint, dram or glass is indeed one of our favourites. It brings with it the chance to chat to strangers, dance like madmen (and women!) and go 'on the pull', three of our other favourites!

Edinburgh has always had a broad range of pubs and bars – some still operating today have been virtually the same for generations. But like all cities, the scene has changed with the times. In the nineties, we saw the growth of the theme pub, led by a major influx of Irish Bars, or 'Plastic Paddy Pubs' as a friend once called them. Their legacy remains today, with those Irish bars still sitting beside 'eerie', ethnic and music theme bars throughout the city.

In the last five years, Edinburgh has gradually seen a major gentrification of its watering holes, with many old locals being gutted and re-fitted as upmarket pre-club venues, café bars and wine bars. Most recently, we've had the advent of the Superbar or ClubPub, where large bars also have dance floors and DJs to compete with the pay-at-the-door venues.

Happily though, the good old quality drinking dens are still holding their own. If you're after a quiet nip of a 30-year-old malt or a pint of Heather Ale, you'll find it all here, along with plenty of loquacious locals prepared to talk your hind leg off! Every pub has its own character, style and atmosphere, so you'll easily find a pub you'll be happy to call your 'local' for the duration of your stay.

So, with all that in mind, if you're in need of a light refreshment, here's our guide to where to find it:

OLD TOWN AND BRIDGES

Logie Baird's Bar
1 South Bridge   556 9043

In the Bank Hotel, right at the corner of the Bridges and the High Street, sits a large, central wooden bar surrounded mainly by standing room only. Logie Baird's always seems to be full of sports fans (in my experience anyway).

Funnily enough, this is a converted bank building and the inside structure has been described as a bit like a waiting room. However, it is a popular city centre venue, with a decent range of beers and if you have a few too many, you might be able to get a night in one of the hotel's various Scottish-themed rooms.

Room 399
The Scotsman Hotel, 20 North Bridge   556 5565

New on the scene, as The Scotsman Hotel (on the site of the old Scotsman Newspaper publishing offices) is, Room 399 is already getting itself well known. The main reason for this is that it's a good place to find and try whiskies you may not get to see in most other bars. If I explain that 399 is not part of the address, but in fact the number of different bottles they have available for sipping, you might understand why.

Whistle Binkies
4-6 South Bridge   557 5114

This is the late night venue of choice for those who don't want to stop drinking after 1:00, but don't really want to go full on clubbing either. This is evidenced by the fact that it becomes quite a sweaty squeeze later on at weekends, with some blaring tunes and a relatively cramped dance floor.

If you're looking for somewhere for a great deal of human contact, and some serious drunken abandon into the small hours, this is the place to come. If you're looking for an intimate nightcap – best avoided…

Iguana
41 Lothian Street   220 4288

Classy, stylish and with their own in-house lifestyle magazine, Iguana has aimed itself firmly at the young up and coming set in Edinburgh. You'll need to look good and bring your plastic to spend the evening here, because it ain't cheap. The décor is a mix of wrought metal and wood and the tables are pretty unique – see for yourself.

It's still in the heart of studentland, so there's an element that harks back to its previous student bar days, but, well, you get the idea…

Greyfriar's Bobby Bar
34 Candlemaker Row   225 8328

Well, if you've managed to come to Edinburgh without hearing of Greyfriar's Bobby, then you haven't been paying attention. Short version of the story: owner dies, dog sits at his graveside for 14 years and earns freedom of the city. For the longer version, see the big Hollywood adaptation with singing children et al, or pick up a book in any local bookshop.

If visiting the pub, which is a bit of an Edinburgh legend in its own right, is not enough, you can admire the statue of the loyal canine outside the pub, or pop round the back to Greyfriar's Kirkyard, where the dog kept his unusual watch.

Beluga
30a Chambers Street   624 4545

Another of the nouveau riche of Edinburgh's bars, Beluga manages to fuse modern and elegant with an industrial pipe kind of feel to create its own unique atmosphere, a sort of futuristic chic. The drinks range is upmarket and so is the clientele. This is a big, underground venue, which seems to attract a slightly older, mid twenties and upwards, crowd compared to some of the other city centre venues. There's also a separate restaurant upstairs, which I hear good things about, but have yet to try myself.

Bannerman's
212 Cowgate   556 3254

I don't know anybody who has been to this pub who doesn't have an affection for it. The walls are all pure old stone and the vaulted shape comes from the fact that…it used to be vaults. I personally preferred it when they had a series of mammothly long tables and accompanying benches across the room, but the comfy chairs and wooden tables are not a bad second.

The draft beers here are usually good quality, the music is pretty universally appealing and depending on the night of the week, you can expect live music, a DJ or a quiz.

Siglo
184-186 Cowgate   240 2850

Talk about turning from a caterpillar into a butterfly – this used to be "The Green Tree", a dingy pub with a little beer garden famous for serving anyone over the age of 15. Nowadays, only the beer garden remains the same, with the pub having become a brightly coloured, neon party bar. As I understand it, they pride themselves on their "jugs" and their cocktails, and there are TV screens galore. Basically, a place to drink and have fun at the same time.

The Three Sisters
139 Cowgate   622 6801

One of Edinburgh's biggest successes in recent years, the Three Sisters is actually three different pubs rolled into one. Based on the story of, believe it or not, three sisters whose lives took very different tracks, the bar has a modern American style section as you enter, and changes to a gothic and then Irish theme as you move through to the back bar. There's also their own club floor called 'Upstairs @ the Three Sisters', which is one of the few pub clubs that actually has a large dance floor. The music is mostly chart stuff. Then there's the massive outdoor beer garden in the front and a pretty decent food menu (with the sisters' story on the back), all of which has blended to make this one of Edinburgh's premier nightspots, so go early if you hope to get in without queuing.

Abbar
73 Cowgate   225 1757

I hate this pub. Why, then would I recommend it to you, you might ask? Well, the reasons I hate it are twofold: One, it used to be "Sneeky Pete's", one of my favourite pubs, with a cracking jukebox and a good atmosphere (although the draft beer was dodgy). Two: I hate Abba. The reason I recommend it is this: it is a pretty good 70's theme pub, as I understand them, and if that's the kind of thing you're looking for, this is probably where you'll want to go. But don't expect to find me propping up the bar – I'll be next door in…

Opium
71 Cowgate   225 8382

This is one of my personal favourites. This place has been through more variations on a theme than I can remember, but now, it has become what Edinburgh has been lacking for years, a good quality, upmarket, rock theme bar that serves good Guinness!

The jukebox covers everything from classics to current Nu-Metal, there are a couple of (slightly cramped) pool tables and a second floor upstairs that opens later on to become a mini club with DJ and a rather cramped "mosh pit". If this is your idea of a night out, Opium is the best place to go and stay out until 3 am. Only thing wrong with it is I miss the roaring open fire of its "Legends" days…

The Halfway House
24 Fleshmarket Close   225 7101

Turn off near the top of Cockburn Street and head directly down to Market Street on Fleshmarket Close and you'll come across a couple of pubs in a truly unique Edinburgh setting. The building that houses the intimate little Halfway House is centuries old, and has spent much of it as a pub. Previously called Benett's, it hasn't even clocked up 100 years yet under its current name! There's even a brief history lesson on plaques outside the door.

The tradition here is for good malts and ales and if you're lucky you might even get some home-cooked Scottish fayre too. Haggis, stovies and soup; pretty much what you'd have been served a few hundred years ago…

Jinglin Geordie
22 Fleshmarket Close   225 2803

Just a few steps up the close from the Halfway House, is the other of this unusual pair. Operating for a century now, this was formerly known as The Suburban Bar

after the nearby suburban railway. "Jinglin Geordie" was the nickname of George Heriot, Royal Goldsmith, Pawnbroker and Money-lender for James VI at the start of the 17th century. Heriot's touch is elsewhere in Edinburgh, his legacy of a hospital for poor orphans was merged with the Watt Institution in 1885 to form Heriot-Watt College, now a flourishing University on the south side of the city.

Another small premises, the offer here is a range of Belhaven beers and premium lagers, with prices lower than the usual city centre standard. Again, a comfortable, traditional feel in an unusual setting.

Frankenstein
26 George IV Bridge   622 1818

The "Established 1818" claim of this huge gothic theme bar refers not to when the pub opened, but to when Mary Shelley penned and published her story about the dangers of man's search for immortality. Sprawling over three floors of a converted church, this building was a theme bar in waiting until Saltire Taverns took it over and created a homage to the monster in 2000. If that's your kind of thing, this is a fun place to drink.

The usual city centre mix of bottled beers, alcopops and spirits is on sale and there's a pretty good food menu covering traditional pub grub, curry and some Tex-Mex Char grill too. They're also big on sports, so if you want to catch some local action without standing around outside, they've got 2 big screens. In the new tradition, they have a DJ every night. And of course, if you've never drunk a cocktail from a test tube, this is the place to experience it first.

Biddy Mulligan's
94-96 Grassmarket   220 1246

Named, I assume, after the titular "buxom fine widow" in the traditional Irish ballad of the same name, this is one of the better and larger Irish themed bars in town. Always busy, usually with students, I remember them starting their business life a few years back with T-shirts proclaiming "Everybody has to learn to drink somewhere", which pretty much tells you where they're pitching themselves.

You'll get a good pint of Guinness here, and usually a good pint of Irish ale too (my memory tells me it's Kilkenny) and some standard fare lunches at decent prices. You can sit outside in the summer, or in the big windows to watch the world go by.

Maggie Dickson's
92 Grassmarket   225 6601

Immediately next to Biddy's, is Maggie's. Maggie Dickson was one of the few victims of a Grassmarket hanging to survive and live out a long and healthy life. Having being found guilty of hiding the death of her illegitimate child, she was hanged, pronounced dead and then found to be alive on the way to her grave. Having been pronounced dead, it was considered unseemly to hang her again, so she lived out the rest of her natural life as "Half-hangit Maggie".

Deservedly, after that, she has a permanent memorial in the form of her very own theme pub. There are a lot of hangman's relics on the wall, as well as a recount of her story, but this is also a friendly pub with good beer and a pretty good jukebox. I, myself, have galumphed about like a fool to The Pogues' "Sally Maclennane" through the back after a few beers. There used to be a pretty good pub quiz of a Monday night, but I haven't been in many years, so it may well be defunct now.

The Black Bull
12 Grassmarket   225 6636

If you're a little older than the average student, and looking for a good point, this a fine place to spend the evening. As with many Edinburgh pubs, the décor is mostly wooden and this is a truly huge split-level traditional Scottish drinker. We took a friend here for his stag night and got him so sozzled on the bottled beers that we lost him for several hours, only for him to turn up at 5 in the morning, having hitched his way home to Dundee. I don't necessarily recommend you follow his lead.

There's also, occasionally, live music on here and they have a great menu – particularly good is their Sunday brunch, if you need a fry up to get over the night before.

Deacon Brodie's Tavern — 435 Lawnmarket — 225 6531

The famous Deacon Brodie: possibly the most ironic figure in Edinburgh history. Upstanding, law upholding citizen by day; by night he put on a mask and robbed people blind, inspiring Stevenson to create the famous Dr Jekyll and Mr Hyde. Why was he ironic? Because when they caught him, they hanged him from the gallows, the very thing he had been designing a replacement for!

This pub has survived a long time on a turnover of tourists coming back from the castle, but nowadays its good range of drinks and a decent upstairs restaurant attract quite a few MSP's from the temporary parliament across the road, so if you fancy a bit of politician spotting…

Ensign Ewart — 521 Lawnmarket — 225 7440

The first pub you come across as you head east down from the Castle, this is an absolutely great little pub. A more welcoming atmosphere you won't find anywhere in town and if you're looking for somewhere that leaves you feeling like you could just about put your slippers on, this is the place. Set in a lovely old stone building, the Ensign Ewart is named after a heroic young soldier who captured the French Flag at the battle of Waterloo.

The drinks here are very traditional: ales and malts, and there's often a wee folk musician sitting in the corner by the bar for your entertainment – and he's most likely just a local who has wandered in with a guitar, rather than paid entertainment!

The World's End — 4 High Street — 556 3628

This is an award-winning pub and deservedly so for the quality of its beer and its pub food, so that, in itself, should be enough to send you in for a visit. If it's not, then there's a lot of interesting history to go with it. Now, some locals will tell you that it's called the World's End after two young women disappeared sometime in the 60's/70's and that the last place they were seen was in this pub. There's also a tale of an evil old Laird who used to live at this site, who famously had jet-black hair and a flaming red beard. Supposedly, the last man the girls were seen with in the bar…had black hair and a red beard.

But it's all hooey. Rubbish. I think there might actually have been a couple of girls who disappeared after being in there, but that's all the truth there is in the matter. Actually the pub is called the World's End because it lies at what was once the border of the Old Town. If you look outside on the street, you'll see little brass plates in the cobbles that mark where the Gate used to be in the Flodden Wall, erected to keep out the English, back when they kept trying to sack the castle.

Tolbooth Tavern — 167 Canongate — 556 5348

Set near the site of, you guessed it, the old Tolbooth, this pub can trace its roots right back to 1557, apparently. It is better known locally for the ghosts that have apparently hung around for a few centuries, occasionally knocking things over for show. Now that kind of loyalty in a regular any pub would kill for!

Holyrood Tavern — 9a Holyrood Road — 556 5044

Just up the road from the impending Scottish Parliament building, you'll find a little pub called the Holyrood Tavern. Well, it looks little on the outside, but it

goes a long way back! This is a real "comfy pub" – right down to the sofas. Purpose built in 1898, the tavern has traded continuously ever since and nowadays offers a range of good real ales and malt whiskies.

It is a very friendly venue and the clientele crosses all borders – while not a gay bar, they are "gay friendly" – basically, everyone is welcome, and you'll feel it. This is one bar where I think I've always been served with a smile and, usually, a bit of banter. Also, since the demise of Sneeky Pete's (RIP), it has one of the better jukeboxes in Edinburgh.

The Royal Oak — 1 Infirmary Street — 557 2976

Next door is the antithesis of modern and trendy. The Royal Oak has long been known for it's unsophisticated charms, which are, in order: 1/ It's one of the last places in town you can get into for a drink until the wee small hours, 2/ The clientele is genuinely eclectic and crosses all borders, 3/ There's usually a little hairy bloke with a guitar somewhere in the smoke filled haze downstairs warbling folk tunes, which get less and less coherent as the ale takes effect, and 4/ The beer's not bad and the staff are quite friendly.

Apparently there is an upstairs bar here. I say "apparently", because I've never been in it, always heading straight downstairs for that great atmosphere. If you're even remotely in the vicinity, you must stop in for a late night drink – you'll never forget it!

Club Mercado — 36-39 Market Street — 226 4224

One of Edinburgh's top clubs and the place many locals go when they're out in their "pulling pants". Fridays are "Time Tunnel" night, playing 60's – 90's pop, while Saturday is "Eyecandy", a glam house night. Oh, and once a month, Sunday sees "Tackno", which is the best of, well, cheesy tack, really and a bit of an Edinburgh institution. Prices are standard clubland, with bottled beers and alcopops and entry is from £5 upwards, depending on the night.

Espionage — 4 India Buildings, Victoria Street — 477 7007

Well, it's another one of those that has taken an old favourite of mine away. This used to be 'The Mission', where I misspent most of my 18th year on Friday and Saturday nights. In fairness though, what they've done here is probably the most impressive of the lot. Espionage is, wait for it, a spy theme bar (check out the phone number!). Set in a labyrinthine old building (which may actually have been a mission at some point?), there are four different themed levels, called Lizard Lounge, Kasbar, Pravda and Mata Hari. But that's not the whole story. See, when I said bar, what I meant was "Superbar". This was the first and still the largest enterprise, which is essentially a massive club with no entry charge. It has a capacity of almost 1000 and at my count, three separate dance floors to strut your stuff on. That's if you can move of course, because it gets extremely busy and sweaty. In fact, a friend recently commented that she felt very old in there because all she could think of was: 'What if there was a fire?'

Finnegan's Wake — 9b Victoria Street — 226 3816

Well, if it's named after one of James Joyce's impenetrable novels, it must be an Irish bar. The difference is that Irish people actually drink in here, so going by the Dublin rule, that you never order a pint of Guinness before checking to see if the locals are drinking it, this would seem to be the best place to get a taste of Eire in Edinburgh.

Of course, the live music every night probably doesn't hurt to attract a people renowned for their ability to party, and the size of the place means there's always room for one more, so if you're looking to taste a bit of the craic while you're here, you know where to stop in. Try to make it in the evening though, if you're looking for a party; it's quieter during the day.

The Liquid Room
9c Victoria Street   225 2564

The Liquid Room has always been one of the "cool"(sic) places to go, whether for a club night or a live gig. It's underground, sweaty and not decorated at all, particularly, so it has a bohemian charm if that's your thing.

The club nights here cover all, from student to garage, so phone to check out what's on when you're here, and if you fancy some live music, this is a pretty good place to get it.

Hogshead
30-32 Bread Street   221 0575

A slightly odd one this, as the Hogshead chain has gone for a manufactured traditional feel, which actually works. This particular venue was once a warehouse, but now has been translated into one of the bigger pubs in the area, frequented by all shapes and sizes of clientele. The reason for this may be that all shapes and sizes of drinks are offered here, including a large range of cask ales, whiskies, and even the odd cask cider.

The Hogshead also has a pretty good pub menu of hearty, stick to your ribs fare, so you can easily satisfy hunger here as well as thirst, without getting bored. In fact, if you had a mind to, you could easily spend an evening here without having the same drink twice!

NEW TOWN AND STOCKBRIDGE

Baroque
39-41 Broughton Street   557 0627

If you're perhaps missing Barcelona while you're here, you could stop in for a drink at Baroque. The tiles, colours and metal furnishings are all reminiscent of the great Antonio Gaudi, leader of the Spanish Art Nouveau movement, whose influence covers the Catalan capital.

Drinks wise, there's a range of cask ales, bottled beers and wines and the clientele is mostly twenty-somethings, particularly at the weekends, but there are exceptions to that rule. There's also some decent grub on offer, if you're peckish, or just don't want to waste time leaving the pub for things like food.

Cask & Barrel
115 Broughton Street   556 3132

There is absolutely no question why this pub is in here; because they serve very good cask conditioned real ales. And there are also some interesting imports and, believe it or not, mead. It's pretty much a men's old-fashioned drinking den of a place, with a big central wooden bar and a plethora of regulars who would most likely die rather than drink elsewhere. However, it still attracts a cross section of society, including a fair number of tourists. Friendly and good quality, this is where guid honest Scotsmen come tae drink.

The Barony
81-83 Broughton Street   557 0546

An old fashioned name for an actual, genuine old-fashioned pub. This is what a Victorian pub looks like when it's left alone and they concentrate on selling good beer. I can personally vouch that the Guinness is excellent here, and that the nachos are pretty good too. There's no telly here, it's really all about good drink, good food and a nice atmosphere. Top pub.

Hogshead
22 Rose Street   226 1224

Much like it's sister in the West Port (see Old Town section), except down in a basement off Castle Street. Brick walls, wooden furniture - it's a hearty pub and, being where it is, fills up quickly at weekends.

Smithies Ale House
49-51 Eyre Place   556 9805

This is a really cool little pub, if for no other reason that it is the only gas-lit pub in the city! Not that it retained the lights, the pub's not that old, but it has gone for a Victorian feel, which may not be as authentic as The Barony, but it works nonetheless. Good ales and beers – a small venue, but friendly staff, prepared to chat over a pint. I think there are quite a few regulars from the nearby Leith Agency, who came up with the brilliant Irn Bru adverts you will probably see around now and again, so you never know what creative juices might rub off.

Po Na Na Souk Bar
43b Frederick Street   226 2224

A Moroccan style underground club, which has become extremely popular with trendy city centre clubbers. Again, it's pretty sweaty, but it's the "in" hangout for the beautiful ones to dress scantily and gyrate to chart and dance music. Gets extremely busy so don't arrive too late or you may have to queue in the cold for some time…

All Bar One
29 George Street   226 9971

All Bar One is a chain of bars that all seem to inhabit massive buildings. The décor is natural stone walls, high ceiling, long wooden benches in the main body of the room and a few alcoves just as you come in for those who want a bit of privacy. The bar is huge, so even when it's busy you should be able to make your way to it. Good range of the usual high street beers and a decent wine range at high street prices. There's also a massive blackboard at the end of the room listing the food available that day, all of which is pretty well done and well presented. Basically it's all very civilised and I'm sure the bankers of days gone by would approve…

Bar 38
126-128 George Street   220 6180

I used to end up here quite a lot for after work drinks on a Friday night, because my wife used to work around the corner. It's a very modern style bar, but still comfortable, with some cosy booths for four to six, as well as central wooden tables. Famously launched itself with an Ally McBeal-style communal toilet, but actually, there's a girls' side and a boys' side and all you really share is the metallic fountain thing for washing your hands in. Still – it's a bit unusual. Drinks are, again, city centre usuals – no cask ales, lots of bottled beers and alcopops. There's a tapas style food menu, which is not bad, either for lunch or fending off hunger while drinking and you can even get table service if you're particularly nice to the staff.

Grape
13 St Andrew Square   557 4522

Another quick Ally McBeal reference: this wine bar is located in the ground floor of "The Capital Building" which makes it a lot like the bar in said programme. However, this being Edinburgh, instead of being full of lawyers, it's full of financial sector workers. Good range of wines, this is positioned firmly in the upmarket, young to middle aged professionals market, so if that's where you like to relax and unwind after a hard days holidaying…

Opal Lounge
51 George Street   226 2275

This is a late addition to the guide, only having opened recently. The Opal Lounge is absolutely massive, with five different rooms done up in a very classy Oriental style. The subdued lighting adds to a very foreign feel in general. This place almost has split personalities, but it manages to combine restaurant, bar and club into one being. During the day you'll mostly find people eating from the Oriental themed menu or drinking the extravagant cocktails, while at night it becomes a real drinking haven with a lot of dancing going on and even some parties who have food shoved out for them too! A real 'happening' place, where the wannabes and the wanna be seens like to get together.

Whynot?
The Dome, 14 George Street

Another underground venue, this trendy club is part of The Dome and caters to the same upmarket crowd. The revolving spotlight logo on the pavement outside gives it a feel of Hollywood celebrity and it has its charms in that direction. Again, though, it's a hot one, being underground and the music is chart and dance. Expensive, but attracts the appropriate crowd for it.

Jekyll & Hyde
112 Hanover Street   225 2022

Here's another Old Town / New Town parallel: while the Old Town has an old bar named for Deacon Brodie, the New Town has a new bar named for the book he inspired. Part of the same "Eerie" pub family as Frankenstein's, this is a smaller but equally gothic venue, with a real flame burning outside and the "seven deadly sins" cocktails available at the bar. The gimmick here is a good one: the toilets are hidden behind a wall with a mock bookcase on it and you have to figure out where they are and which one's which. Most people just cave in and ask for help…

The Northern Bar
1 Howard Place   556 1558

Located just along from the Botanic Gardens in a very picturesque little area, this is a friendly local bar with good service, friendly clientele and a pool table. Spent many days here during one particular Edinburgh Festival, thanks to one of our cast living round the corner, and pretty much made it our own for the week. Good place for quiet drink out of the centre, or to stop into for a rest after walking the Botanics.

Kay's Bar
112 Hanover Street   225 1858

This is a very nice, upmarket but traditional pub, priding itself on the very high quality of its cask conditioned beers and malt whiskies. It also does a solid menu of home cooked fare for lunch and the clientele tends to heavily lean towards regulars, which can't be a bad sign about the quality of the place. The reverence with which these regulars discuss the bar make it an essential visit if you're anywhere nearby.

The Star Bar
1 Northumberland Place   539 8070

One of those Edinburgh pubs everybody seems to have been to at least once, I like it very much. This may have something to do with my becoming friendly with the locals and bar staff thanks to a friend who technically lives next door, but seems to spend more time in here playing fusbal (table football) than he does in the house. Very friendly, easy going place, there's a communal guitar open to anyone who fancies having a strum and also chess behind the bar, which you would apparently be well advised not to challenge Emma the barmaid to, unless you enjoy losing.

The Conan Doyle
71-73 York Place   524 0031

Named for Arthur Conan Doyle, creator of Sherlock Holmes, this corner pub sits opposite the statue of the master detective, which looks to be modelled on Basil Rathbone, in my opinion. (The last time Hibs won a trophy, Sherlock found himself wearing a Hibs scarf and a cone on his head!) This is a large, wooden décor bar, modelled on the sitting room of Holmes himself, with good food and a large screen telly that shows all the major sports events, which tends to focus on football, in case you haven't noticed. Crowd is fairly young and sporty and drinks range pretty much the standard.

Breck's
110-114 Rose Street   225 3297

Named after Alan Breck, the highlander from Stevenson's "Kidnapped". Basically a comfy pub, good beer and wine and a solid bet for a bit of convivial company in town. Met a mate from school here working behind the bar, on the day before he was emigrating to Australia, so you never know what serendipitous experience you might have. This place looks great in the summer when all the flowers in the hanging baskets outside are in bloom.

Dirty Dick's
159 Rose Street   225 4610

What a name. Owned now by the same company that runs The Bad Ass, they've turned it into another nice eaterie bar, that is quite upmarket, despite the name. Pleasant staff, decent beers, another safe bet for a pleasant time, especially if you're peckish.

Great Grog
43 Rose Street   225 1616

Owned, I believe, by the same company that runs the wine home delivery service, this is an unusual beast – a wine bar with a casual atmosphere and no pretensions. So, if you're more of a wine-quoffer than a beer-swiller but would prefer to avoid some of the snobbishness that often comes with it, here's your answer.

Scott's Bar
202 Rose Street   225 7401

One of the leading lights of Rose Street and rightly so. Apparently, the landlady here some years ago was the infamous "Ma Scott", who jealously guarded her till and promptly removed anyone who caused a stir. Good range of beers and worth a seat in the sun outside, weather permitting, as it so rarely does! Commonly frequented by sports fans, particularly rugby when international games are on.

The Abbotsford Bar
3 Rose Street   225 5276

An architecturally significant bar, The Abbotsford has remained much the same since the early 1900's. The large central bar is ornately carved from Spanish mahogany and it has an intricate plaster ceiling too. Named after Walter Scott's baronial mansion, The Abbotsford carries a good range of beers and also offers a good place to stop for a hot chocolate when shopping has your feet giving up the ghost, as I can testify.

Yo Below
66 Rose Street   220 6040

The bar half of the Yo! pair is underneath Yo Sushi. Very modern and, I guess, Japanese in décor, the main thing that is interesting about this place is you serve yourself beer from the T shaped taps on the tables and pay at the end. Now, I have so far avoided this as I'm sure it could lead in all kinds of dangerous directions, not the least of which being a heavy hangover to go with a large overdraft, but it has a novelty and convenience factor that exemplifies much of what the Japanese are about: technology that is fun.

Hectors
47-49 Deanhaugh Street   343 1735

All glass and manners, this upmarket bar in the heart of Stockbridge would be a major pre-clubbing venue, if there were any clubs nearby. As it is, I imagine there are still a number of social butterflies who pop in here for a G&T or an alcopop before heading up into town to dance the night away and look beautiful.

Raeburn House Hotel
112 Raeburn Place   332 9469

A small hotel set in a lovely old Georgian house. The main attractions here are that it is in a lovely area, family friendly and also offers some decent food, so you can sit outside in the garden on a nice day and let the kids play while you sup and eat to your heart's content. Expecting to expand in the near future onto the rugby pitches behind the building.

The Bailie
2-4 St Stephen Street   225 4673

I was introduced to The Bailie by someone who said: 'Ohmigod! You've never been to The Bailie!', and that pretty much sums up the feeling of adoration its regulars have for it. A good old pub with a quite sophisticated and slightly bohemian clientele, you could be forgiven for people-watching here as there are some characters worth seeing. In pub terms, it is a lovely big basement pub, with a central bar in dark wood. There's no music, just general chit chat, good beer and some great pub grub to entertain you. A quite unique place to visit if you're nearby.

Harvey's
39 Thistle Street   478 7029

Formerly known as "The Howff" which basically means Scottish drinking den, this pub was re-named after the film starring Jimmy Stewart and an invisible six-foot rabbit. That in itself is enough to sell it to me, but Icelandic proprietor Eirny Sigurdardottir has also taken the advice of one Elwood P Dowd from that same film: (and I misquote) "In life you can either be oh so clever or oh so pleasant. I recommend pleasant" and pleasant this place is, with friendly staff, a beer garden and, among the selection of drinks, Icelandic spirits. Another one of those unique places with a lively clientele, and possibly, a polite rabbit that will open the toilet door for you.

The Cambridge Bar
Young Street   225 4266

There's something to be said for the fact that we have a Cambridge Bar and an Oxford bar in such close proximity in Edinburgh – seems we're trying to initiate our very own "boat race" (which, for those not in the know, is also a type of drinking race between two teams). The Cambridge Bar, with quality real ales

available as well as good food, has a traditional Scottish pub atmosphere. They also used to be big American Football fans, supporting the Scottish Claymores – not sure if that's still the case…

The Oxford Bar
8 Young Street   539 7119

The Oxford Bar on the other hand is at least a little bit famous. It has a long reputation for being the haunt of Scottish writers, and is currently the watering hole of choice of Ian Rankin, author of the Inspector Rebus mysteries. There's a well stocked bar and a wealth of regulars who seem absolutely dedicated to their pub, so it might be worth finding out why while you're here…

WEST END AND LOTHIAN ROAD

Caley Sample Rooms
58 Angle Park Terrace   227 7204

A large, quite traditional feeling pub, this was once owned by the nearby Caledonian Brewery, but is now a separate entity in its own right. Basically, as you'd expect, it is best known for its ales, which you can stand at an old barrel to drink. Very popular with Hearts fans, with Tynecastle Stadium not far away.
This is a good place to meet before hand or retire to after if you're thinking of touring the Caledonian Brewery, which is just up the road. It also gets a special mention particularly because the manager of my dearly departed Leith Oyster Bar is now the manager here, so when you're in, say hello to Donald and tell him I sent you!

The Caledonian Ale House
1 Haymarket Terrace   337 1006

Similar name, different pub. The Caledonian Ale House is often referred to as the Callie Ale House, mainly to confuse tourists, I suppose. This is a totally different pub, attracts more of the rugby crowd than the football, especially before an international at Murrayfield. Nice marble floors, as I recall (not having been in for a while) and very upmarket décor places this a bit further up the economic food chain from other similar real ale pubs, but that's probably what attracts the rugger crowd in the first place. It's a more sophisticated type of place to sup your beer I suppose, if a little pricier for the privilege.

All Bar One
Exchange Plaza   221 7951

I won't often give directions, but this one's hard to find. About halfway up Lothian Road there is a large square on the right hand side with the Sheraton at the back and a big Clydesdale Bank building on one side. If you head to the back right corner, you will find an All Bar One tucked away back there. Funnily enough, it attracts the crowd from these nearby offices. I don't know why, maybe it's the big glass windows or the fact you can easily sit outside, or even the slightly hidden nature of it, but I like this pub better than its sister on George Street, despite them having much the same style, food and bar stock. Ah well, no accounting for taste, eh?

The Citrus Club
40-42 Grindlay Street   622 7086

On my first ever visit to the Citrus Club I felt it was unpromising as I walked in the door. Basically, a couple of concrete corridors lead you to a large concrete dance floor with a concrete balcony round about it. Then I heard the music, which was, I think, the Police, followed by some Ska and then maybe The Wonderstuff and I barely moved from the dance floor for the rest of the night. What I seem to have walked in on was a fairly typical night there, with their very popular Tease Age being the Indie night to die for on a Saturday. Don't remember much more about that or subsequent visits, except that I always seem to dance a lot and get very sweaty in here. Good venue, will usually play something to satisfy everyone at some point.

Uluru
13 Lothian Road   228 5407

Uluru is the Aboriginal name for Australia's favourite monolith, Ayers Rock. In fact, let's be more direct – Uluru is the real name for what later Australians came to call Ayers Rock. Since the whole rock is covered in Aboriginal history and myth it seems fair to say they had it first.

Anyway, this little pub on Lothian Road is probably one of the few Aboriginal themed bars in the country. It's quite plain, really, with a split-level to one end, pool, table football and a relaxed, fairly studenty atmosphere. A good friend of mine who has coerced me in here a few times (coincidentally a student) loves this bar and demanded that I include it, so here it is. OK, Kenny? (Actually, it is quite a fun wee bar – and they do food too.)

Henry's Cellar Bar
8 Morrison Street   221 1288

Jazz. That's pretty much what you need to know about this bar – it's open late and it does a great turn in live jazz bands. For "late" read 3 am and for "jazz" read improvised and highly entertaining, if you're into that sort of thing. Which I am, on occasion, and can say I've had some cracking nights here and can't suddenly think of a single good reason why I don't go more often. Used to have a good excuse as a friend managed a pub round the corner and we'd drink there then pop round to Henry's after closing time – which is what a lot of people do as an alternative to hitting the club scene, I think. Very chilled, very real, man. Yeah. (My fingers are clicking even as I write this.)

Thomson's Bar
182-184 Morrison Street   228 5700

Named after and designed to follow the architectural style of Alexander "Greek" Thomson, the 19th Century architect whose use of classical Greek styling led to his nickname. It is unusual to see a tribute in Edinburgh to a man whose work was almost entirely done in Glasgow, as there is little love lost between the two cities. However, Thomson is only really second to Rennie Macintosh in terms of well-known Scottish architects, so we suppose we're prepared to accept it, under the circumstances.

Not being a scholar of Thomson, I cannot testify to his social preferences, but if this pub is anything to go by, he enjoyed a good clean pint of well-preserved real ale, in a non-pretentious atmosphere. This place has become extremely popular with the local journalists who work around the corner for Business AM, but don't let that put you off!

Indigo Yard
7 Charlotte Lane   220 5603

Indigo Yard is, without a doubt, the place to be seen drinking in Edinburgh. Formed partially by an old courtyard, the bar has a huge ceiling which gives it the impression of being an outdoor bar without the danger of getting your head wet or freezing to death, for that matter. There's a pretty cool melted wax thing going on on one wall and the whole place has a real cool chic about it that attracts all of Edinburgh's wannabes, "are's" and "don't really care because I'm way too cool for thats". Friends and I occasionally play spot the millionaire in here, because it has the kind of atmosphere where you just know there's at least one in the room and it's probably the bloke in the corner in the Marks and Spencer's jumper with the cane rather than they guy at the bar in the Armani suit.

Drinks wise, you'll get all the upmarket standards here – Stella and the like – as well as a good selection of cocktails for the laydees (or the men intent on getting legless after work on a Friday!). There's also a very good, modern menu of food available, with a separate dining area through the back, should you be of such a mind. Apparently the occasional celeb pops in here too, but I've yet to see one.

Mathers
1-3 Queensferry Street   225 3549

I seem to have used the phrase 'Edinburgh institution' a few times already, but none is more deserving than Mathers. Not to be confused with its namesake on Broughton Street, this is the Edinburgh bar where locals go for a damn good pint or malt whisky and no messing. Operating since 1903, this old style bar retains almost all of its original features and is known for the good atmosphere generated between regulars and visitors. Many a man will go out for an evening and 'end up in Mathers' because it seems to have that magnetic effect that says, 'you're guaranteed a good time here'.

SOUTHSIDE, TOLLCROSS AND MORNINGSIDE

The Meadow Bar
42-44 Buccleuch Street   667 6907

Known familiarly as the 'Moo Bar', this is a really studenty pub that also gets some custom from nearby offices (advertising agency and publishing company), which I can testify to, having previously worked in one of those very offices and been in for several pints of a Friday evening. Most notable thing about it really is the large bizarre metal sculptures of animals' heads on the wall. They seem completely incongruous with the surroundings, and yet, there they are. There's also a giant snake. This was one of the first pubs I knew of to sell Absinthe during its recent revival in popularity amongst the Edinburgh pubs. Seats are a mix of sofas, benches and stools that were most likely picked up second hand somewhere nearby. Not a bad little bar, with little the operative word, but worth a drink if you're of that ilk.

Bierex
1 Grange Road   667 2335

Modern and trendy, another Friends style pub. A central semi circular bar is surrounded mostly by booths notched in against the windows, or against the stone at the back. Makes for quite a private drink, really. Again, it's in the student area, so it attracts a few of them, but it also gets the working set from nearby, especially at lunchtime. Decent beer, upmarket atmosphere and pretty good food for lunch too – I had a rather nice steak baguette with blue cheese here quite a while ago and I still remember it fondly.

The Old Bell
233 Causewayside   668 1573

One of those pubs everyone seems to have heard of but not been to, it is a little bit out of the way, but it is also extremely inviting. It's one of those pubs that makes you feel a bit like you've stepped into a world separated from the outside, with intricate woodwork and old fashioned décor just about transporting you back a few centuries. Oh, and there are bells. Several. Hence the name, obviously…

The Abbey
65 South Clerk Street   668 4862

Quite a studenty bar, most of the reason I know it is that my wife and I used to meet here for lunch, as it was halfway between our respective offices and offered the standard Festival Inns menu, which is basically good traditional stick to your ribs stuff, with specials changing daily.

There's a large, square central wooden bar with seats and benches all around, although there's better seating on the south side of the bar than the north side. Drinks are pretty much standard, with a few draughts and the bottled stuff. As I recall, there are also some odd old Scottish sayings painted on the beams that have been put on the ceiling to give it a mock old fashioned feel. Nice place for a bite or a lunchtime tipple.

Native State
32-34 Potter Row   662 9788

This is some pub. It used to be The Woolpack, which was an absolute student standard and most likely named after the pub in British soap opera "Emmerdale". Unfortunately, poor old Woolie's crowds started to dwindle and so Native State was born. It's very much been upmarketed, with metal décor and great big wooden tables sprawling across the centre of the room. There's a wall of pictures of (presumably) famous people, but I've yet to meet anyone who could name them all, or even decide if a few of them were male or female! This was also one of the first bars I've been in to have two flat screen TV's behind the bar playing films to keep you entertained while you wait to be served. I actually saw Toy Story 2 here, before I'd seen it anywhere else!

This is another place that does great food at lunchtime and is extremely busy because of it. In the evening there are still a fair number of more affluent students, but there's also an after work crowd too these days. I happen to know they're quite keen to attract tourists too, so you should expect to find yourself welcomed with open arms, or at least with a good film.

Junction Bar
24-26 West Preston Street   667 3010

I seem to be recommending a lot of bars up here for lunches – can you spot what I often did for lunch when I worked nearby? Of course, we never had beer during the working day – heaven forbid! This is another one for good pub grub, particularly good burgers with curly fries and they do a nice latte to finish you off. Beers range is fairly normal; with bottles being what I usually took with my burger. They always had some sort of special deal on for every night of the week too, like free nachos on a Tuesday between 5 and 7 or some such thing, which were written up on the blackboard in the back bar – see for yourself what they're offering these days.

The Crags
58 Dalkeith Road   667 4518

Been through many incarnations this one. Most recently a Firkin, until most of them were sold off, The Crags retains that slightly anarchic feel while now being a Bass pub. Named for the Salisbury Crags of which the pub has an excellent view, this is popular mainly with two groups: employees of the Scottish Widows (insurance company) across the road, and students, from Pollock Halls, just down the road a bit. The pub itself is pretty huge, with little interesting touches, like cutlery that comes in a little wellie boot and irregular shaped pool tables. The lunchtime faire is basically burgers and stuff and is not bad; beers are Bass and bottled alternatives. I believe they also have in-house student discounts too. There's a massive back room, which has a big screen TV that gets wheeled down for sports games and is the place where I watched the most unbelievable comeback in football history when Man United came back from a goal down to Bayern Munich to win the European Cup in injury time. What a night that was…

The Maltings
81-85 St Leonards Street   667 5946

Very much still a traditional pub, this was recommended to me by a friend I consider an aficionado of two things publike: beer and pub quizzes. They serve Theakston's on tap, which is never a bad thing, as well as the fairly standard range of others and a range of bottles and spirits. It is renowned as a friendly pub and I think is still somewhat of a local for the Police station across the road. The Superheroes painted on a board outside seemed incongruous to me at first, but then they have that kind of laid back, informal atmosphere to suggest anything goes. On all of these bases, I'm going to take my own advice and check out their pub quiz (Seemingly on a Wednesday night) over a few jars in the near future.

Peartree House
38 West Nicolson Street   667 7533

It is slightly serendipitous that this happens to be next on my list, as this is where I rather infrequently already attend a pub quiz of a Monday evening. Hosted by the inimitable Dave, the quiz is great fun, includes a "music" round with audio intros, and lots of other fun stuff. Usually end up quite drunk and out quite late at this, so don't do it too often, since it hinders work on a Tuesday. The pub itself is rather casual and intimate, despite being of a decent size. It's another with a central wooden bar, which is surrounded by dark wooden and leather furniture, but don't get the impression that it is terribly posh. This furniture is more like that inherited by the children of someone who was once posh, who have subsequently used them repeatedly for late night student parties – and it is mostly students and graduates who wish they were still students who drink here, or at least, who attend the quiz here.

Lots of history here, with the building itself built as a residence in 1749 and having many residents die inside, leading to rumours of ghosts still hanging around. There's a large courtyard outside which is now a beer garden, probably the best known in Edinburgh, which is constantly full of people drinking and cavorting when the weather permits. There is also, of course, the Pear Tree after which the house is named, with the 250-year-old beast still bearing fruit to this day, apparently…

The Blind Poet
32 West Nicolson Street   667 4268

Part of the same building as Peartree House, this is named after a former resident of the building, Dr Thomas Blacklock, who had visitors of the calibre of the famous lexicographer, Dr Johnson and our national bard himself Rabbie Burns. Up on the first floor (or the second floor, for Americans) this is another student bar, but also a decent venue for catching bands, when they're on and in particular I've enjoyed a few evenings of good live jazz here, but sadly it's been too long since the last time. In fact, so much so, I'm now going to put some on in the background while I continue to write the rest of this section. Quite a moody little bar, I think, it has that kind of atmosphere that suggests everyone there is part of some conspiracy and is privileged to be there. Or maybe that's just me.

Bennet's Bar
8 Leven Street   229 5143

I can't find anything but people saying great things about this bar. My colleague told me 'You must include Bennet's', my student friend said 'I take it you've got Bennet's in' and the various reviewers whose material I have perused for background information say things like: 'one of the finest pubs on the planet" and 'a real gem'. So if you don't like this, there's something wrong with you.
This is an extremely well preserved Victorian pub, which is entirely listed as a result. There are many original fittings, which have been well looked after, notably brass water taps on the bar and a small 'snug' bar for more private service. (No not that kind of private service). There are several cask ales on offer and a large selection of malt whiskies too. Due to its proximity to the King's Theatre, there is also a separate room through the back called the 'Green Room'.

Burlington Bertie's
11-13 Tarvit Street   229 8659

Quite a unique little pub, this one. Staying with the theatrical theme of the area, this is named after a Music Hall character from the early half of the 20th Century. Created by Ella Shields, who was an early cross dresser and inspired the Victor/Victoria film starring Julie Andrews, Burlington Bertie was "a penniless Londoner who affects the manner of a well-heeled gentleman". Bertie him/herself can be seen in the bar on several mirrors.
The pub is extremely small, but also usually full, even during the week. There's no messing about here, the point is to drink and smoke in a convivial, if dark

atmosphere. The beer range is good, with cask ales on tap as well as several lagers and beers, wines and the usual spirits. A regular crowd includes students, theatregoers and locals, but there's a welcome for like-minded visitors too. It's also open late to get as much drinking in as possible. Like I said, no messing…

Cloisters
26 Brougham Street   221 9997

This is an extremely cool pub. Set in an old manse (the minister's house, from the church next door), it retains very much a religious and ancient feel while still providing a modern atmosphere for drinking in. The walls are stone, the seats are wooden benches, and even the bar has a solid, sacred feel to it that makes the whole experience unique. Drinking is given the reverence it deserves here with a good selection of ales and malts and the clientele is very mixed, up to and including after work drinkers from near and far. In fact, the first time I was ever here was on a work night out, and I instantly fell in love with the place. Not for the highly religious type, opposed to holy ground being tarnished though…

Belfry Bar
1 Barclay Place   221 0291

Known affectionately as 'The Batcave' by my student friend, this is a nice modern bar, popular with students and locals (many of whom are students in this part of town). Several things worth mentioning here: The staff – apparently also extremely good, I was regaled with a story about arriving early and wanting to sit in the small beer garden, so a single table and chairs were put out specially, while the rest of the bar was set up. The beer garden itself is apparently not that well known, but small and nice for a seat outside in the sun. The toilets – OK, won't often make mention of these, but then it's not many toilets that will play cartoons at you so you can be entertained while you tinkle.

Beers wise, there are a few cask ales alongside the regulars, plus some cocktails on offer. It's fairly quiet during the week, but heaving at weekends.

Golf Tavern
30 Wright's Houses   229 1093

If you fancy a bit of golf as well as a bit of beer, you can come here to rent some clubs from the golf tavern and have a round on the pitch and putt course out on the Meadows before coming back to quench your thirst. The Golf Tavern is another well-preserved building, listed and dating back to the mid 18th Century as licensed premises. The beer is some cask ales and the standards, while the regulars are, again, mainly students but also some locals who are loyal regulars. There's a fair bit of golfing memorabilia to be seen here, so if your swinging days are behind you, you can at least come in for a wee nostalgia trip over a tipple.

The Canny Man's
237 Morningside Road   447 1484

A truly unique pub this one. A word of warning, though, if they don't like you, you simply won't be served. I'm not kidding. That doesn't mean you shouldn't try though. Here are some tips, as I understand them. 1/ Dress well. 2/ Don't be too young. 3/ Carry yourself with dignity and show due respect and politeness for the others who have been welcomed into the house along with you, many of whom are regulars who consider this their second home.

If it comes down to it though and they don't like the look of you – give up, there's little point in arguing. Apparently, the standard here is that the owner, the fourth in the family line to own and run this quirky little pub, will only serve those whom he would be prepared to welcome into his own house. Make of that what you will.

Those who are allowed entry will be party to quite an experience. The walls are adorned with all manner of trinkets that have either been given or pledged against drink since the hostelry opened in 1871. Each of the various little rooms has a name as do many of the tables, and your standing amongst the staff and

clientele will dictate at which you will be allowed to sit. There are a number of traditions on the go here, like the "bell board" used for passing out messages and the "four ale notice board". The staff are structured so that you know their rank by their clothing: below the owner, Mr. James Kerr, are: The Suits, The Blazers, The Aprons and finally, The Shirts (who are only there on trial). You have to earn the right to work in this bar and it comes with no small kudos to be offered a permanent place. If you are lucky enough to be allowed to stay, try to find a local regular or staff member to fill you in on the history – it is quite an engrossing story. Before I run out of room, I should mention that the drinks on offer are: Cask ales; several hundred malt whiskies served only with spring water, never tap water; their own blended whisky, 'The Golden Drop'; a few dozen vodkas; gins; wines imported directly from France and Spain and champagnes, served with strawberries. Such touches of class here make this little business so enduring and make many glad that it has long resisted the onslaught of theme bars and brewery owned premises – those of us who are allowed in of course. Oh, and I should mention the food – extremely good, if not cheap, but then, if cheap is all you're after, this isn't for you anyway…

The Merlin
168-172 Morningside Road   447 4329

Well, a hard act to follow and a completely different pub to follow it. Just up the road is The Merlin, formerly a fairly studenty bar, good for watching the football, which has now been completely gutted and obviously "designed" for that trendier look. Light wooden furniture, a clean, crisp look about the bar, glass/metal decor and a square chrome log fireplace carved into one wall are what make this yet another of the gentrified set in Edinburgh. There's a large (purple) pool table and a large screen TV on the raised bit at the back, which is not apparently used for football, so we're not sure what it is for.

Beers are the standards on tap, plus lots of bottled options including the Bacardi Breezer types for the laydees. Clientele is still a little studenty but they've got some of the beautiful ones now as well…

The Waiting Room
7-8 Belhaven Terrace   452 9707

"If we're not in the Merlin, we're probably in The Waiting Room", said my student friend, who then went on to describe it as more of a 'young and trendy' pub than a student bar. The main things I know about this place are: it takes getting drunk seriously, offering cocktails and pitchers of beer as well as some very good bistro style food. So, if you're up that way and fancy an all in one night out, this would seem to be the answer – all you need is a sleeping bag and hey, you don't even need a hotel anymore!

EAST END AND PORTOBELLO

Blind Beggar
97-99 Broughton Road   557 3130

About all you really need to know about this little pub to decide whether or not you want to drink here is this: it's a biker bar. They play loud metal music and there are a lot of people dressed in leathers. I think the beers range is pretty standard, and there's a pub quiz that is fun and attracts a lot of punters in, but of course the music round is fairly predictable. So if your first ever love was your Harley, then this is the pub for you. If not, but you like hairy men in leather and loud music, it could still be for you. If you're more of a sweaters and loafers type of man, I would find somewhere else to drink, if I were you.

Claremont Bar
133 East Claremont Street   556 5662

Again, the main reason I mention this pub is not so much what they serve, but what goes on here. This is a real cult culture pub. They're into Star Trek, Rocky Horror, Fortean stuff and all the like. There are groups that meet here regularly and the clientele is quite mixed, as it's a fairly gay friendly atmosphere. If you're into any of the above, you might want to give them a call and see what's happening while you're in town. Beers, again, pretty standard.

Sheep Heid Inn   43-45 The Causeway   656 6951

Those of you who have come to Edinburgh looking for some old world charm and have found many of the pubs on offer a bit too modern should make your way to Duddingston Village. It is one of the quaintest little places you'll find anywhere in the world, nestled just off the south side of Arthur's Seat. The Sheep Heid Inn is the oldest surviving pub in Edinburgh, with a Tavern having been here for at least 500 years! It is named after a snuffbox given to the Inn by James VI, son of Mary Queen of Scots, who also visited the pub, as did, apparently, Bonnie Prince Charlie. Such royal connections will always draw tourists anyway, but the pub itself would be just as great without those tales.

It has a real ambience of history about it and you can still imagine all the past souls who have supped their ale here while on their way somewhere or other. The tavern is beautifully preserved and has the extra addition of a traditional skittles alley (sort of like ten pin bowling) in the back, which can be booked for parties. Basically, this is a great place to stop for a lazy afternoon's drinking, and on a sunny day you can sit out in the beer garden and gaze up at the old volcano.

Theatre Royal   24a-27 Greenside Place   557 2142

This is an absolutely massive bar. It's all done in wood inside and the central, square bar is surrounded by pillars and carved wood decorations. It's also got a big open fire through the back in the winter. Most interesting thing about it though is that it tends to be where the cast of any shows that are on at the Playhouse next door come out and go to for a drink, so worth going in for a post theatre beverage if you fancy a chance of chatting up the leggy blonde from the chorus, for example. They also tend to be very welcoming to opposing rugby fans on international weekends and it's a handy place to meet people, as you can't miss it. Another one that does a decent food menu and you can sit outside in the sunshine, when it comes along!

LEITH

Cameo Bar   23 Commercial Street   554 9999

The Cameo is (alas) all that remains of the once mighty Oyster Bar Empire that had pubs all over Edinburgh. My own favourite and second home for about 8 years was the Leith Oyster Bar, sadly now gone. However, the Cameo is not a bad stand in, with the same friendly and eclectic bar staff, good pub food, including some great nachos and burgers and 'Eggs West Coast', which is basically Eggs Benedict with salmon instead of ham.

There are other attractions here too – regulars play 'ghoul pool', with a pool running bets on who the next major celebrity to 'pass over' will be. There's also a putting green out the back, would you believe, and summer sees mini golf tournaments played on Sundays. The range of beers is fairly standard, with sometimes a few cask ales on, but more often just one. A decent range of wines too, due to the fact that half of the building is taken up by La Camargue, their sister seafood restaurant, which I hear is not too bad at all, but for some reason I've never eaten there, yet. A lot of regulars here and you never know who you might bump into, including occasional ex-lead singers of major rock bands!

Port O' Leith   58 Constitution Street   554 2024

This is an absolute institution and if you want a feel of Leith from its old maritime days that's absolutely genuine, pop in here for a drink. There's no tat on the go here, but dozens of flags from all different countries hanging on the ceiling, given by visiting sailors in port. There's a life-size bust of the owner, Mary, over the bar, who herself is somewhat of an institution.

Absolutely everyone is welcome here and, apparently, people who have been away from Leith for tens of years will still come back for a drink in the Port O' Leith because it reminds them of the Leith they grew up in and left behind. Can't even begin to remember what the drinks range is like, but to be honest, it's not that important, because whatever you drink, it'll be the atmosphere and surroundings you'll enjoy.

Robbie's Bar   367 Leith Walk   554 6850

Known as a good real ale pub, a good friend of mine who worked many years in the bar trade was trained in cellar management here and assured me it was the best kept cellar he'd ever seen before or since – so you can safely bet on a good pint of real ale here. It's also pretty friendly, with a more traditional Scottish pub look both inside and out.

King's Wark   36 Shore   554 9260

I took a decision at the beginning of this guide to only feature any given company under one section, and this is one of those that gave me a real headache deciding where to put it. The King's Wark is a lovely old stone bar with décor in dark wood which, by candlelight of an evening is an excellent place to drink in a convivial but also private atmosphere – there's almost a conspiratorial feel about the place and you can easily imagine yourself as a pirate or some such a few hundred years back in time as you sup your beer. Scenes from Treasure Island could be set here.

However, it also has a small separate room, which is a dedicated restaurant and serves some excellent fresh fish and shellfish, so I did agonise over whether it should be in the eating section. In the end, I thought about what I think of it as, and I drink here semi-regularly but have only eaten here a few times, so that made my mind up – and I certainly hope they won't mind my choice!

Malt & Hops   45 Shore   555 0083

I have a lot of personal history in this pub. Several friends have worked here, I've seen good friends play gigs here, I've sat outside drinking after work on some glorious summer days and I've huddled near the open fire to warm up on cold winter nights. That's all because it's basically a very friendly, welcoming, cosy bar, with a good rotating selection of ales, which are well looked after. In particular they tend to stock less well-known Scottish ales and often, Fraoch, a Scottish Heather Ale. Again, many regulars here and even a regular dog who is extremely friendly to anyone. And they serve chilli nuts, which is a bonus in my book.

Old Chain Pier   32 Trinity Crescent   552 1233

Built around the original stone anchorage of the Trinity Chain Pier, this is a lovely old-fashioned pub that looks like it was cobbled together in pieces over the years. In fact, it was rebuilt on the site of an older pub that was in danger of falling into the Firth of Forth that it overlooks. If you don't sit too near the window, you could easily convince yourself that you are in fact afloat at sea.

There's a couple of real ales here on offer and the food also has a good selection and is good quality for a nice lunch. If you're remotely into such things, this pub is almost warren-like and has absolutely bags of character. Great fun.

The Starbank Inn   64 Laverockbank Road   552 4141

An excellent ale pub, with equally good views out over the Firth. I can honestly say one of the best and most refreshing pints I've had in recent memory was the pint of Ossian's I had here not long ago. Food is a good menu and not bad quality, with particularly friendly service from the very nice lady who serves it. If you like good views, a traditional pub feel and damn fine real ale, pop out here for a visit.

entertainment

If you find yourself puggled with sightseeing, you may want to do something else with your day. If you're in the mood for a film, a show, some sports, whether watching or doing, or just something a bit more unusual to do, there are plenty of options to choose from here. So, without further ado, here is our guide to Edinburgh's most entertaining things to do…

OLD TOWN AND BRIDGES

Dynamic Earth   112-116 Holyrood Road   550 7800

This is our equivalent of London's Millennium Dome, except that ours is not being turned into a car park after a year. It is in fact a highly educational little trip, worth doing at least once no matter what your age, but particularly worth repeating if you've got kids, as there are lots of things to play with and see, including experiencing a volcanic eruption, a slightly nauseating trip through the Antarctic surrounded by real ice and a rather impressive rainforest with moving creatures. It can be a little frightening for the under threes when the "time machine" elevator takes you down, but the rest should love it, especially the early stuff with the primordial soup and the farting noises!

Edinburgh Dungeon   31 Market Street   240 1000

When I was wee, there was a wax museum on the High Street, which had all sorts of famous figures, much like Madame Tussaud's, and at the end you came to a junction, at which you could either leave one way, or enter the "Chamber of Horrors" the other way. Why you would want to leave was beyond me - as a ten-year-old boy that was the bit I was most looking forward to seeing. Then it closed down and a while later the Edinburgh Dungeon opened at the West End. Now it has settled on Market Street, taking you on an underground boat tour through Edinburgh's dark and grisly past. Now, if that had been available as an option when I was ten, good lord I'd never have been out of the place!

NEW TOWN AND STOCKBRIDGE

The Stand   5 York Place   558 7272

If you want to see the beginnings of Scotland's next big comedians, this is the place to come. I was introduced to this little comedy bar by a Canadian friend I used to work with when he was first doing stand up here and he went on to win the BBC's New Comedy Awards last year (or was it the year before?). Anyway, there's usually always something on here and there's a bar and some food to have while you're watching some of the acts, and I think they even do a comedy pub quiz, so you've got plenty of options…

Easy Internet Café   58 Rose Street   220 3580

Well, it pretty much does what it says in the name – lots of terminals with Internet access so you can check your email while you're away from home!

WEST END AND LOTHIAN ROAD

Edinburgh Zoo   134 Corstorphine Road   334 9171

Edinburgh Zoo is set on a hill slope out on the Airport road. It's an excellent zoo, as these things go, and is particularly famous for its penguins and they have a regular 'penguin parade' which really excites the younger kids watching. Call to find out when the parade is on…

Megabowl   Fountain Park   478 9999

Ten pin bowling with all the side attractions to keep the family happy, including pool tables, a fast food burger joint, a bar for the adults and sweetie machines. Family day out easily planned and held under one roof!

UGC Cinema   Fountain Park   0870 902 0417

One of the newest multiplex cinemas in Edinburgh, this one has all the luxuries – seats that give you plenty of room and a cup holder at either side, great quality sound and the ability to pay for everything, including popcorn and drinks, with plastic! Modern cinema going for the convenience generation…

Laserquest   56 Dalry Road   346 1919

This is one of those war game things which I'm sure are terribly unhealthy but a hell of a lot of fun too. They've just moved to these new premises and I haven't been since then, but the premise is basically: run around with a pack on your back in a room full of dry ice smoke and shoot at the other people. Lots of fun, but be warned – there's a particularly nasty warden who bellows at anybody caught breaking the very strict rules and it can be quite irritating having someone younger and a lot smaller than you bellowing "Stand UP!" at you in the dark…

The Caledonian Brewing Co   42 Slateford Road   227 1286

We're quite proud of this little brewery, producing as it does some cracking beers, which have won many awards and, frankly, taste great. You can take a tour of the brewery and sample some of the product at the end, which I highly recommend. You'll then more than likely go home and immediately start looking for a pub that sells "Caley 80".

Midlothian Ski Centre   Hillend   445 4433

It's a fair old way out of town, but if skiing is your thing, we've got an all year round dry ski slope for you. I have been once in my life, fell over and hurt my shoulder and decided I was never going skiing again. True to my word, I haven't. But I'm a clumsy oaf who hates both the cold and pain, so don't let that put you off!

Filmhouse   88 Lothian Road   228 2688

Our best arthouse cinema and the home of the Edinburgh Film Festival. This has two screens and a great little restaurant. The films on show are usually either classics or hard to see independent films. Call for film times.

Royal Lyceum Theatre   30b Grindlay Street   248 4848

There are three major theatres right next to each other here. The Lyceum tends to be the most traditional and mainstream of the three, to my mind.

Traverse Theatre   10 Cambridge Street   228 1404

The Traverse, on the other hand, tends to show more modern and unusual stuff.

Usher Hall   Lothian Road   228 8616

And I always associate the Usher Hall with classical music and orchestras. Of course, I could be completely wrong (but I don't think so), so just call to see what they've got on or, again, stop in for a programme.

Murrayfield Ice Rink   Riverside Crescent   337 6933

You can either ice skate or watch an ice hockey game featuring the Edinburgh Capitals.

SOUTHSIDE, TOLLCROSS AND MORNINGSIDE

Festival City Theatre   13-29 Nicolson Street   529 6000

The Festival was recently created from the remains of an old theatre and it's been a huge success. They tend to put on just about everything: theatre, ballet, musicals, opera and anything else they can think of!

Odeon Cinema   7 Clerk Street   0870 505 0007

The only surviving old style mainstream cinema in town. It's got a nice little bar upstairs, which is much better since they unblocked the windows. This kind of comes under the little guy against the big boys, except that Odeon is a national chain, plus this is popular with the students in the area, so it's more of a convenient theatre, if lacking in the multiplex razzmatazz.

EAST END AND PORTOBELLO

Edinburgh Playhouse
18-22 Greenside Place   0870 606 3424

Yet another grand old theatre, this one tends towards musicals more than anything else. (which might account for the number of gay bars and clubs in the immediate area, I suppose!)

Meadowbank Sports Centre
139 London Road   661 5351

Built for the Commonwealth Games, this is an excellent athletics stadium, but you can see more than athletics here. There's also football from local lower league side Edinburgh City and basketball from the Edinburgh Rocks. And there are facilities that you can use if you so desire, like a gym, badminton courts and outdoor Astroturf football pitches.

LEITH

Kinloch Anderson   Dock Street   555 1390
This is a long established kiltmakers, but their Leith store has something a little bit special, a museum called: 'The Heritage of Kinloch Anderson', which is an exhibition featuring the Royal Tartans, kiltmaking and regimental and civilian uniforms as well as over a century's worth of historic items and paintings.

Leith Waterworld   377 Easter Road   555 6000
This is not really a swimming pool, more of a playing pool designed for younger kids to splash around in and have a ball – water with fun, basically!

Ster Century Cinema   Ocean Terminal   553 0700
This is the newest of Edinburgh's Cinemas (at least until the new one at the top of Leith Walk opens!) and it's as space age as I've ever seen. Escalators to different floors and a Ben & Jerry's stall and great big seats and plenty of legroom. Great Stuff.

Scotch Malt Whisky Society
The Vaults, 87 Giles Street   554 3451

Now this is not so much a tour or museum, but an exclusive club for members. However, what they will do is, if you phone to ask first, take you on a wee tour of the building and explain the benefits to you of becoming a member of the Society, if that's something that might interest you. So if you love malt whisky…

Royal Commonwealth Pool   21 Dalkeith Road   667 7211
If you want to go for a swim, then this is the biggest pool we've got. One Olympic size pool is complemented by a kids' pool, a diving pool, and some flumes (water slides). If you want to get wet, this is a good way to do it!

Cameo Cinema   38 Home Street   228 2800
The Cameo falls somewhere between art house and mainstream and it is a lovely old cinema with many charms. It has a nice little bar and probably the comfiest seats in any cinema ever. Always supporting the artistic film world, every feature is preceded by a short independent film.

King's Theatre   2 Leven Street   529 6000
A grand old lady of the theatre world, the King's is a treat to visit. This tends to be Theatre with a capital T, like Shakespeare and Arthur Miller, and pantomime come Christmas time.

Dominion Cinema   18 Newbattle Terrace   447 4771
This is absolutely the coolest little cinema in the world. It is lovely, family run and has not one but two bars, from which you are welcome to take drinks into the cinema with you! They sell all the usual yummy foods plus exotic chocolates and it's just great. Oh yeah, and there is a dinky little cinema with only about thirty seats and a mini screen which I saw Amelie in last year and it is really great!

Festival City

Here is a brief guide to the 10 major festivals held annually in Edinburgh in chronological order from June 2002 to June 2003 and starting with the six different festivals that make August the busiest month in town.

EDINBURGH INTERNATIONAL JAZZ AND BLUES FESTIVAL
26 July – 4 August 2002

World leading jazz and blues musicians come to Edinburgh for 10 days and play for some 50,000 people in bars, concert halls, clubs, streets and parks around the city in the longest running jazz and blues festival in the UK. This is a great time to be wandering the streets, especially if it's sunny, because as you pass many bars you'll hear the sounds of some wonderful music drifting tantalisingly out into the street, making it impossible for you to pass by without at least popping in briefly to bathe in the beat.

For more information or to order a programme, contact: Edinburgh International Jazz and Blues Festival, 29 St Stephens Street, Edinburgh, EH3 5AN. Tel: 0131 225 2202.

EDINBURGH MILITARY TATTOO
2 August – 24 August 2002

The Tattoo is Edinburgh's big annual military celebration. Up on the Castle Esplanade every August, the massed ranks of various military bands perform to the delight of packed audiences, including a small fireworks display and a haunting finale from a lone piper. This year's Tattoo, in celebration of the Queen's Golden Jubilee year, will feature the largest pipes & drums band from Scotland and the Commonwealth ever to appear on the esplanade; Tri-Service Bands of the Royal Marines, the Army and the Royal Air Force; the Bands from 'Down Under'; Commonwealth Highland Dancers and many other acts from around the world. It is quite a spectacle. Performances run from Monday to Friday at 9pm and on Saturdays at 7.30pm and 10.30pm. Tickets range from £9.00 to £27.50.

For more information or to book tickets, contact: Edinburgh Military Tattoo, 32 Market Street, Edinburgh, EH1 1QB. Tel; 0131 225 1188.

EDINBURGH FESTIVAL FRINGE
4 August – 26 August 2002

The Fringe is officially the largest arts festival on the planet, and it breaks its own record every year with increasing participants and attendances. The Fringe has many aspects, but mostly it is about all levels of performers, from the absolute amateurs of community drama groups, to semi-professional and even some professional performers appearing in all aspects of the performing arts: theatre, musical, dance, opera, comedy, children's entertainment and anything else that you can imagine. This year there will be over 16,000 performances of 1350 shows in the 200 converted halls, churches, schools, bars and small theatres that act as the Fringe's venues. Many famous and soon to be famous people have appeared on the Fringe, like *Friends* star David Schwimmer, whose directorial debut was in Edinburgh, alongside all those who are just in it for the love of the experience. During this time, you will find the High Street closed to traffic and absolutely teeming with performers putting on impromptu performances and handing out leaflets to encourage you to visit their shows.

The Perrier Comedy Awards have also become a main feature of the Festival, with The Gilded Balloon and The Pleasance being the two main venues for up and coming comedians. There are two major one off events that punctuate the Fringe every year. **The Cavalcade** kicks off the Festival on the 4th, with a massive parade of floats along Princes Street, featuring many of the companies and venues that will appear around the city in the weeks ahead. **Fringe Sunday**, on the 11th, is a big day out in the Meadows, on the south side of town. Again, many of the companies and acts performing will be out in force and there are several stages on which to see some of the more organised acts. There's also face painting and children's entertainment.

For more information or to order a programme, contact: Edinburgh Festival Fringe Society, 180 High Street, Edinburgh EH1 1QS. Tel: 0131 226 0026

EDINBURGH INTERNATIONAL BOOK FESTIVAL
10 August – 26 August 2002

The gardens of Charlotte Square play host every year to the world's biggest public book event. Publishers from all over the world display their titles in the big tents set up here and many authors themselves will visit. Some of the literary giants appearing in 2001 were Gore Vidal, Doris Lessing, Ian Rankin and P D James, who held one-hour sessions with audiences. There were also some literary themed artistic objects and events, which expanded the whole event. There is always a large amount of children's literature and the event attracted a record number of visitors in 2001, with 120,000 people coming to browse or participate in events. If you're of the type that loves books, then you really have to come and lose an afternoon here, or even just have an impromptu picnic in the park.

For more information or to order a programme, contact: Edinburgh International Book Festival, 137 Dundee Street, Edinburgh, EH11 1BG. Tel: 0131 228 5444.

EDINBURGH INTERNATIONAL FESTIVAL
11 August – 31 August 2002

The International Festival has been running since 1947, bringing the cream of the world's art communities to Edinburgh to perform. All acts appear strictly by invitation of the Festival Director and use all of Edinburgh's major theatres and concert halls for the duration of the event. The events cover dance, music, opera and theatre at the highest level, as well as many discussion forums and lectures about the performances. The whole event culminates in a spectacular annual fireworks display above Edinburgh Castle on the 31st. Highlights of the 2002 Festival will include Wagner's *Parsifal*, conducted by Claudio Abbado and staged by Peter Stein; Jon Fabre's *Swan Lake*, performed by The Royal Ballet of Flanders; Stravinsky's *Oedipus Rex* with Symphony of Psalms by the Canadian Opera Company, directed by Francois Girard; Wagner's *Siegfried*, performed by The Scottish Opera; and Britten's *The Turn of the Screw*, directed by Luc Bondy.

For more information or to order a programme, contact: Edinburgh International Festival, The Hub, Castlehill, Edinburgh EH1 1BW. Tel: 0131 473 2000

EDINBURGH INTERNATIONAL FILM FESTIVAL
14 August – 25 August 2002

Edinburgh's answer to Cannes is not that far below its French cousin in International Film circles. Many European premieres are held here and some of the film world's more hard-to-see gems and unique independent visions will also find their first screenings here. Around 6 cinemas throughout the city participate in the event, showing a wide range of films, which, this year, will include French director Francois Ozon's murder-mystery-musical *8 Femmes*, featuring Catherine Deneuve and Emmanuelle Beart, and Mike Leigh's newest release, *All or Nothing*, starring Timothy Spall.

Full details of the 2002 programme will be available from July 12. For more information or to order a programme, contact: Edinburgh International Film Festival, 88 Lothian Road, Edinburgh, EH3 9BZ. Tel: 0131 228 4051.

EDINBURGH'S CAPITAL CHRISTMAS
15 November – 24 December 2002

A recent addition to the festivals calendar, the winter festival is a treat for those who love the Christmas season. Among the major attractions are a huge Ferris Wheel erected on the south side of Princes Street, an ice-skating rink in Princes Street Gardens and a wonderful German Christmas market along the top tier of the Gardens. In 2001 we even got a toboggan run! You can indeed walk in a Winter Wonderland.

For further information, contact: The Hub, Castlehill, Edinburgh EH1 1BW. Tel: 0131 473 2000.

HOGMANAY
29 December 2002 – 1 January 2003

Hogmanay is what we Scots peculiarly call New Year's Eve. Even we're not sure where the name comes from, with several theories prevalent, but suffice to say that what it means nowadays is a great big party with lots of alcohol and glitter. Edinburgh's Hogmanay party has been voted as among the top 5 parties in the world and the Times called it the best Millenium party in the

world after the 2000 event. The big features are a torchlight procession down the High Street a few days before, then on the night itself, there are various concerts including one in Princes Street Gardens, but the major party is up on Princes Street, where you have to buy a ticket just to get anywhere near the city centre! The big climax of the night is when the fireworks go off all over Edinburgh. If you can stand the cold, this is another of those once-in-a-lifetime experiences that only Edinburgh offers.

For more information, contact: Hogmanay Box Office, The Hub, Castlehill, Edinburgh EH1 1BW. Tel: 0131 473 2000.

EDINBURGH INTERNATIONAL SCIENCE FESTIVAL
4 April – 15 April 2003

Every Easter, Edinburgh celebrates the modern world of science and technology in an effort to spread the knowledge around. With a wide programme of events for adults, children and schools, the Science Festival can help open the minds and horizons of everyone. There are loads of hands on and interactive events for the kids and adults can find themselves face to face with the world's most brilliant scientific minds. 120,000 visitors find their way around the various events each year at the world's first and largest festival dedicated to science.

For more information or to order a programme, contact: Edinburgh International Science Festival, Roxburgh Court, 323 High Street, Edinburgh EH1 1PW. Tel; 0131 220 1882.

SCOTTISH INTERNATIONAL CHILDREN'S FESTIVAL
26 May – 4 June 2003 (to be confirmed)

This is Britain's biggest performing arts festival for children, with shows aimed at kids from 3-12. The point of the Festival is to encourage children to broaden their own horizons and introduce them to new ideas and, of course, to theatre itself. The 2002 event featured international shows from 6 countries and 33 family performances, with free crèche facilities, child friendly venues and even some signed and audio-described performances. This is a great experience for kids and one they're never likely to forget!

For more information or to order a programme, contact: Scottish International Children's Festival, 45a George Street, Edinburgh EH2 2HT. Tel: 0131 225 8050.

Haunted Edinburgh

Edinburgh was built upon a unique geological feature: A large rocky outcropping with a tail made of sandstone, protected by the rock from the onrushing glaciers of the ice age. Edinburgh Castle formed the centre point for the town to grow up along either side of this sandstone ridge, running all the way down the hill to the site where The Palace of Holyroodhouse now sits. During this evolution, the city has seen more blood and torture, devil-worship and witchcraft and ghosts and ghouls than just about anywhere else in the world. Here are the best stories to come out of that history and the places where you can still find traces of these events today:

CRIME AND PUNISHMENT

Historically, it was a bad idea to commit a crime in Edinburgh. At one point in time, there was something in the region of 200 crimes that came with the death penalty in the city. Among the last to suffer this sentence were two juvenile boys named Mair and Aitchison, who, in 1818 were hanged for the terrible act of…housebreaking. But to some, death was a simple and more lenient punishment than they could hope for.

Witness the Mercat Cross. The one which now stands in the High Street, at the entrance to St Giles Cathedral is not the original cross, that having been, for some reason, torn down many years ago. Though perhaps it is best that this is so, since the cross had seen so much blood and pain as to be certain to be haunted nowadays were it not long since consigned to dust. A common practice for petty criminals (beggars, for example) was to be dragged to the Mercat Cross and have their ears nailed to the door for a proscribed period of time that was deemed fitting for their crime. Often they would also be forced to carry a sign that told passers by of their crime, so that they could suitably deride the offender. Many others were hanged here or burned at the stake, but Edinburghers were often at least civilised enough to strangle them first, so that they were not alive when they burned…

However, the punishment itself was often not enough for the city's elders. Prevention was the key to good crime control, which was rife in the Old Town, where overcrowding and squalor were endemic. To that end, many criminals were beheaded and had their heads left on spikes around the walls of the city, so that no one else would think to copy their crimes. This aim was served to in extreme in one case. In 1605, Francis Maubray was charged with treason against the crown. During an unsuccessful attempt to escape his prison cell in Edinburgh Castle, Maubray was killed. End of case, or so you'd think. But a royal warrant was in force here and although Maubray had denied all charges in life, there were witnesses against him and his attempted escape was deemed even more incriminating. Thus was his cold and lifeless body dragged into court, where a trial took place, witnesses were called and sentence was pronounced upon the corpse. Found guilty of treason, the body was duly hanged and quartered, with the pieces staked around conspicuous places in the city. Not even death was enough to escape justice in Edinburgh.

Of course, if treason was considered the worst crime, actual regicide, or murder of the ruling regent, definitely carried the harshest penalties of all. James I left his throne somewhat unceremoniously when he was assassinated near Perth by a group led by Robert Graham, grandson of Walter, the Earl of Atholl. It seems Walter had been told by a group of witches that he was to be king of Scotland, and he hadn't the patience to wait his turn. (Where have I heard that story before?) So, next in line was, of course, King Walter I – not quite. The Earl and his grandson were quickly discovered as the perpetrators of the crime and their punishment was doled out with gusto. Graham, the actual murderer, had his hand nailed to a gallows, which was transported on a cart, with Robert dragged behind it, through the city. The executioner spent the entire journey sticking red-hot iron spikes into various fleshy parts of his body, before he was eventually beheaded and quartered. Would that Walter had been so lucky. As the brains behind the operation, his fate was to be much more grievous.

On the first day, he was attached by rope to a crane, which repeatedly lifted him by his ankles and allowed him to drop back to the ground. Broken bones and dislocated joints obviously followed. On day two he was pilloried and then crowned with a red-hot iron bearing the inscription 'The King of Traitors'. This was as close as he was to come to royalty. Then they attached him to a horse's hurdle and dragged him through the streets, like his grandson. On the third day, he was stretched out and while alive and awake, drawn open and had his vital organs removed before his eyes and thrown onto a fire. His head was then cut off and displayed around the town, while his body was quartered; with one part remaining in Edinburgh while the other three were sent to Perth, Stirling and Aberdeen. Bet old Walter regretted his lack of patience in the end, ay?

Of course, had the people of Edinburgh believed the treatment to be unjust, chances are it never would have happened at all. You see, throughout the ages, the Edinburgh Mob became one of the most notorious and most feared throughout Europe, and woe betide he who committed an injustice in their eyes. If a criminal was deemed to be undeserving of punishment, or a man set free who was guilty in the eyes of the people, the 10,000 strong Edinburgh Mob would be out in numbers to enforce their own justice, before disappearing back down the closes to their homes. There are no real records of who the organisers of the mob were, but history holds the name of one leader who held control of the mob between 1770 and 1780 – Bowed Joseph, a deformed cobbler whose drum could call forth the full strength of the mob in what seemed like a heartbeat. Joseph was no terrorist, but a man with a social conscience who would never let a piece of unfair legislation pass without the mob marching on the city chambers to let their wrath be known. The council even took to appeasing Joseph with ale in advance of announcing legislation they considered controversial. He was also a terror to local landlords who overcharged their tenants and market dealers who were forced to sell their wares at much reduced prices in times of financial hardship. However, all that ale was to prove Joseph's undoing, as he fell from a stagecoach, drunk, on the way home from Leith one day in 1780, dying from his injuries.

To give you a true taste of the Edinburgh mob's power, it would be best to recount a few of their 'adventures", or rather, their accomplishments. In June 1561, a small group decided to perform the play 'Robin Hood' which, against their knowledge, had been banned by law for some years thanks to the Reformation' changing morality. Magistrates descended on the play and removed some props, but these were quickly returned when the mob became restless. In a show of defiance, the magistrates arrested James Gillon, identified as a ringleader, and tried him on the false charge of stealing 10 shillings. A gallows was erected for his execution, but that was as far as it went. The mob moved into action, destroying the gallows and chasing the magistrates down the High Street to the Tolbooth Prison, where Gillon was held. They then broke into the prison, set Gillon free and replaced him with the magistrates, who were forced to remain there until the evening, when they acceded to proclaim that no one would be prosecuted for the preceding events.

Easily the most famous event in the Edinburgh Mob's history though, surrounds the infamous Captain John Porteous of the City Guard and what came to be known as the Porteous Riots. Porteous was a poor choice to lead an unpopular force. He was arrogant, outspoken against the mob and boasted of his friends in high places. He was never going to win any popularity contests. In 1736, ten years after his appointment, the animosity came to a head over the case of two smugglers, one of whom, Wilson, sacrificed himself so that his partner, Robertson, could escape justice. Now, smuggling was seen as a somewhat romantic crime in these days, perpetrated by loveable rogues, so Wilson's selfless heroics had made him a popular and heroic figure with the mob – and Porteous intended to put him to death.

On the allocated day for the execution, the city's leaders feared the mob would run riot and had made all the preparations possible – the entire City Guard was on active duty with guns and ammunition ready and a detachment of solders at the ready if required. Porteous blamed Wilson for this terrible insult to the City Guard's capabilities to deal with the mob. In malicious revenge, he squeezed Wilson's wrists into manacles far too small for him, causing him to cry out in pain – word of this torture spread quickly through the amassed crowd. In the face of the assembled military might, the crowd were quelled and stood silently while the execution took place, but afterwards, all hell broke loose. Stones were hurled at Porteous and the guards as a relative of the deceased rushed forward in an attempt to resuscitate him. Porteous then opened fire on the crowd, which the rest of the Guard followed him in – killing three outright and wounding over a dozen, including those hit by stray bullets while watching out of their windows. The Guard then marched away, leaving the dead in their wake. The furious mob followed them up to West Bow, where more shots were fired and another three killed.

As a result, Porteous and thirty men were removed from their positions, and Porteous was to be tried for murder, but managed to avoid it on the basis that he was acting on orders from the city to keep the peace. Porteous was still sentenced to death for ordering his men to open fire unjustly, though. Porteous' 'high friends' then took action and got him a reprieve direct from Queen Caroline. The Mob didn't care – they wanted him dead. And so it was that on the 8th September 1736, they locked the city against reserve forces, marched on the Tolbooth to retrieve Porteous and took him to the Grassmarket, the site of his crime, and hanged him. Many believed that the plan was so well executed that some noblemen had been involved in the event, dressed as members of the mob, for Porteous' unpopularity crossed many class borders, but regardless, Porteous was dead and the mob had made their power clear.

One of Edinburgh's most famous ghoulish stories also involves the mob, but only peripherally, for it was what happened in their absence that was the real 'meat' of the story. In 1707 on the night of the signing of the Treaty of Union, Queensberry House, residence of the Duke of Queensberry, played host to an event legendary in Edinburgh's grisly folklore.

To say that the Treaty of Union, which passed control of Scotland's political affairs over to England, was unpopular with the Edinburgh Mob would be quite an understatement. The whole event was being pushed through by noblemen like the Duke of Queensberry who were being very highly rewarded for their betrayal of Scotland's desires, with both titles and silver aplenty pouring in. The people of Scotland had not forgotten the past raids by, and wars with, their southern neighbours and had no desire to be in union with them. Thus it was that, when news spread that the treaty was to be signed that night, the Mob took to the streets, roaming the city in search of the signing place, so that they could forcibly stop the event. Knowing this was likely to be the case, Quensberry took his entire house staff with him for protection, bar one young kitchen boy, left to tend to the roast on the fire, which was to be their feast when they returned home, triumphant.

However, what they returned home to, after betraying their nation, was a terrible and macabre sight. For the Duke had an idiot son, long since believed dead, who had been imprisoned in a darkened room since a young age and had grown to a much larger than normal man, described as a 'giant'. With his normal guard away with his father, the son had escaped his prison and found his way, by hunger and his nose, to the kitchen. There, he had discovered the roast and the terrified boy and, finding the roast unsatisfactory, he had flung it aside, murdered the boy with his bare hands and was busy feasting on his partially roasted body when his family returned. And they say karma takes its time to get you back…

This is just one of Edinburgh's truly famous stories, of which there are a few. You may for example have heard of the Hellfire Club, but not known from where the name comes. It was in Edinburgh that a group of nobles used to congregate in the depths of the South Bridge vaults and partake of depraved debauchery, drinking and the occult. And of course, there was Maggie Dickson, mentioned in the drinking guide, who was hanged for concealing her pregnancy to the son of her employer and trying to hide the child's death days after his birth. She survived the hanging, but having been pronounced dead, it was deemed improper for her to be hanged again and thus she lived out a long life as 'Half-hangit Maggie'. Speaking of people with pubs named after them, there is also Deacon Brodie, the upright citizen who took to crime to pay off his gambling debts and to help keep not one, but two mistresses, and who was eventually hanged to death despite many precautions he had taken in advance to 'cheat the wuddie", or survive the gallows – he lived on only as the inspiration for Stevenson's 'Jekyll and Hyde'. But as our subject here is the macabre and grisly history of Edinburgh, it seems only fitting that we recount in some detail the story of two of Edinburgh's most famous residents: Burke and Hare.

Both christened William and immigrants from Ireland, they separately became navvies on the Union Canal before ending up in Edinburgh in search of work and their fortune. They met in 1826 when Burke and his long-time 'companion", Helen McDougal, moved into Mrs Log's Boarding House in Tanner's Close, where Hare was already resident. After the death of Mr Log, Hare took up with the merry widow Log, and the four who would perpetrate some of the worst murders in Edinburgh's folklore were together.

In November of 1827, 'Old Donald", a long time resident of the guesthouse, died owing £3 in rent unpaid. At this time, it was illegal to use bodies for medical purposes in the country, but many were still required for training and research, and so the occupation of the 'body snatchers", or 'Resurrectionists' came to be, where graves would regularly be robbed of their freshly buried contents and sold to doctors for about £10. Burke and Hare are often referred to as 'the grave robbers", but this they were not, for none of their victims ever made it as far as the graveyard before they took them.

Knowing that Old Donald's body was worth more than the rent he owed, they arranged to replace the corpse in the coffin with bark, and carted the poor cadaver off for sale to Dr Knox, of Surgeon's Square, for £7 10 shillings, a good deal more than he owed. The ladies then suggested that the two should take up the Resurrectionist game, but Burke had other things in mind. He had no interest in the dirty, sly work of grave digging, when he could just get to the bodies earlier. So it was that when another tenant took ill in the lodgings, failing to pay rent and also scaring off other guests, Burke talked Hare into assisting while he suffocated the last dregs of life out of the poor fellow and placed him in the tea chest for transportation to Dr Knox, where £10 was procured for the fresh corpse. The body snatchers had become murderers.

Now, though, there was a conscious decision to be made. There were no more dead or dying making themselves readily available to the pair, which meant that if they were going to carry on in this game, they were going to have to start drumming up their own business. So it was that Abigail Simpson became their first real prey in February of 1828. The old woman was lured to their lodgings, gotten blind drunk and then suffocated to death in their now familiar manner, whereafter £10 was procured from Dr Knox for her corpse. Next they went for a younger victim, Mary Haldane, an experienced prostitute, whose body was worth even more than the previous-best £10.

Seeing that the better the bodies were, the more they were worth, Burke and Hare became arrogant and indiscriminate in their murders. In April 1828, young prostitute Mary Paterson was murdered. But the murder was bungled and her friend, Janet Brown, allowed to escape the scene prior to the act. Mary, though, was not so lucky and was soon paid for by Dr Knox. However, her body was absolutely perfect and renowned throughout the underworld, so much so that one of Knox's students even recognised her, but Knox saw only a flawless subject, and even had an artist record her lifeless body before she was dissected.

What followed was a horrific reign of terror upon the streets of Edinburgh, while the pair, led by Burke's ego, murdered their way through the Edinburgh underworld, taking the daughter of Mary Haldane to join her mother, an old Irish woman and her deaf mute grandson in one swoop, and Burke even killing a horse that refused to carry some of their macabre cargo to the doctor's for them.

A row happened between the two when Hare took it upon himself to kill and sell an old woman while Burke was on holiday, which resulted in Burke and McDougal moving out of the lodgings. But the murderous partnership was to continue. The pair killed Helen's cousin Ann on a visit from Falkirk and they were back at it again, killing unknown numbers of victims before they started to make mistakes too big to be missed.

The murder of Daft Jamie, a well-known local idiot, was one, but the worst was that of Mrs Doherty. Being so arrogant as to keep her body in a room where guests who had seen her the night before came in and found her, the couple went straight to the police, against Helen's vehement pleas for mercy.

Their trial took place on 24 December 1828, but only Burke and McDougal were tried, as Hare and Log turned state's evidence in return for a pardon of their own parts in the crimes. Burke was sentenced to death, while McDougal's verdict was the peculiarly Scottish 'not proven'. On 28 January 1829 Burke was hanged before the amassed Edinburgh Mob, who demanded the same of Hare, thus causing him to flee the city forever, until he died destitute in a cellar in London, having been blinded in a previous narrow escape from death in a limekiln when his identity had been uncovered. And that was the end of Edinburgh's most famous murderers, Burke and Hare.

THE RESURRECTIONISTS

Of course, while not murderers, there were a few stories of famous body snatchers to be had around the time too. The most well known were a band led by 'Merry Andrew", an unusually tall and gaunt man. His trio was made up by the physically and mentally deficient 'Spune' and the mercenary former plasterer, 'Moudewart'. These three were infamous for their antics and their colourful characters among the medical fraternity, who sometimes even took it upon themselves to play jokes on the trio, telling them of dead bodies where the poor 'victim' was still very much alive. In one case, however, a set of body snatchers found that this could be the case, even in extreme circumstances.

Greyfriar's Kirkyard was the scene of many a stolen body, so much so that relatives would often post a constant vigil at the graveside of a recently deceased relative until they were sure it had decayed enough to be of no use to the snatchers. It is said that one night, a group had dug up the body of a recently deceased old woman and found her to have been considerably wealthy, with a number of valuable rings on her hands. As was their wont, the ghouls began the task of removing the jewellery by cutting off the woman's fingers, but as the first cut was made, the woman sat bolt upright in her coffin and screamed in pain! She was not dead at all, but accidentally buried alive, having been in a trance like state. Sadly, this was not an uncommon occurrence in the days of less advanced medical science, and many coffins have been subsequently uncovered with terrible scratches and gouges on the inside of the lid, where the occupant had clearly awoken to find themselves six feet under…

DEVIL'S ADVOCATES

All of this was, of course, rooted firmly in the world of the physical, if somewhat grisly. There are parts of Edinburgh's past, however, that go far beyond those bounds. Devil worship and witchcraft were very much feared in these times and anyone suspected of the black arts was more likely than not to find themselves at a stake or the end of a rope before too long. Visions of Satan himself, or Auld Clootie as he was known, were not unheard of. On the eve of the battle of Culloden, one man claimed to have seen Satan reading a proclamation of the names of Scots who would die the next day and soon be in his charge. The man rushed home to make a plea to God for clemency and found himself one of the only men to survive that terrible defeat and live to tell the tale back in Edinburgh.

Many more, though, were those who were supposedly in league with Satan, like the famous North Berwick witches, known for attacking boats at sea as they came in and out of the Forth of Firth. There were four, in particular, though, who were worthy of note. Dr Fian, in the late 16th Century, was sentenced to death for witchcraft after trying to cast a love spell on a young woman he was infatuated with. He was foiled in this by the woman's mother, who apparently caused the spell to affect one of her cows instead, leading to Dr Fian having an amorous bovine to contend with. As if that wasn't enough, a confession was tortured out of him and he was burned at the stake. One of Fian's pupils was Agnes Sampson, who spent most of her devilish powers healing the sick and prophesying the future. This good natured work was apparently not enough to prevent her being tried for witchcraft and conspiring with Satan, and she too was burned at the stake, despite impressing the king with a recount of a private conversation between him and his wife on their wedding night.

Same name, but different witch altogether was Agnes Fynnie, who ran a local market shop and used her powers to put a sickness on those who refused to pay her their dues or criticised her prices and products. Such was her infamy that locals were afraid to cross her in case they should suffer some terrible plague. She too was strangled and then burnt at the stake. And finally, there was Thomas Weir, the Wizard of the West Bow. A retired military man and captain of the City Guard, Weir was recognised as one of the holiest and most upright men in Edinburgh, even earning the name, Angelical Thomas. But behind this mask lurked the private life of a debauched, drunken Satanist, who partook of his many crimes with his sister Jean. He supposedly carried a wizard's staff which was imbued with all his Satanic powers and it was only his conscience which forced him to confess all his evils as he grew older. Despite the attempts of the local clergy to dissuade him, Thomas was adamant he must be punished and he was burned at the stake with his staff beside him. Jean did not go so well, determined to strip herself naked before she fried, it was a battle to see whether she would die before she managed to disrobe entirely. The two could supposedly be seen rampaging around their West Bow flat on occasion, by those with the inclination to see them, until it was destroyed in 1878, since when they are rumoured to have returned to their hometown in Lanarkshire.

GHOSTS OF THE PAST

And that brings us nicely on to our final group of Edinburgh inhabitants, some of whom are still around today – the ghosts. And there are plenty of them.

It is fitting that we should begin with a ghost, or rather an apparition that had a profound effect on the city itself. One

Arthur's Seat, against religious advice to the contrary on the Sabbath day. While out, he was attacked by a marvellous stag and removed from his horse. The great stag was about to finish the job when David grabbed its horns and was amazed to see a large cross appear between them. Being a religious man, he grabbed for the cross to save him…and the stag disappeared. David vowed to build an Abbey of the Holy Rood (or Holy Cross) near to the site of the event, and so he did.

But most of our ghosts are of the human form, and few of them have such holy intentions as the mythical stag.

In 1688, John Chiesly wished to divorce his wife, but could not agree to a settlement that would care for her and their eleven children. He was bound to agree by the decision of the court. Said court, presided over by the Lord President Sir George Lockhart, decided that the family deserved £93 a year from John, a large increase on his preferred option of nothing at all. Feeling hard done by, Chiesly decided to take his revenge on Lockhart and so he did, shooting him through the chest in broad daylight after an Easter ceremony. The Edinburgh Mob came running and Chiesly was carted away to face justice. The justice he faced involved torture to discover any conspirators, and when these were ruled out, his right hand, which held the gun, was cut off and placed on a spike for all to see, while John himself was hung in chains from the Gallow Lee with the offending weapon around his neck. Up until now, this is no different from any other such story in Edinburgh's annals, but this was to have a more interesting denouement. Chiesly's body was removed by an unknown person and shortly after a ghost given the name of One Armed Johnny was found to be rampaging around Dalry, laughing, screeching and screaming. Johnny was seen again and again for three hundred years in the area, until, in 1965, workmen removing a hearthstone in Dalry found a skeleton with its right hand missing and a gun hung about its neck. Johnny's body was properly re-buried and the ghost of Johnny One Arm was never seen again.

Many of Edinburgh's ghost stories revolve around the forgotten passages of the underground city. One such legend centres on a little drummer boy. A passage was supposedly found underneath Edinburgh Castle and the City Council were concerned about the obvious security risk. The opening, however, was extremely small, and thus a young boy (probably used to climbing up and down chimneys, as boys in those days were) was sent into the tunnel to investigate where it led. The elders then followed the boy's drumming from above ground as it led them down the High Street. What they hadn't thought through was what exactly they intended to do if the drumming stopped, which it abruptly did just next to the Tron Kirk. Should they send another boy down to see what had become of the first? What if he met with the same fate?

sacrificing down the tunnel. So the Councilmen, in their wisdom, decided just to block up the tunnel to prevent anything coming out of it, leaving the boy to his presumed fate. Apparently, to this day, on quiet nights, a feint drumming can be heard beneath the High Street just near the Tron, and one tourist in 1994 fainted on hearing the story when in the Kirk, having moments before been wondering what that funny drumming noise she kept hearing was!

During the Revolutionary War in America, one General Robertson of the British Army returned to Scotland with his servant, Tom, who, in less Politically Correct days, became known as 'Black Tom'. They stayed at an ancient house, called Wrychtishousis, as the General's house was being renovated. After their first night, Tom complained of being disturbed by a ghost in the night, specifically, a headless woman carrying a baby who would cross his room from the cupboard and then turn and return to it. Tom begged for another room, but the General, convinced this was the work of drink, refused and forced Tom to stay in his allocated room. For three months Tom begged the General to move him, but he still refused and, eventually, Tom gave in, but his health suffered and he became very thin. Finally, the renovations were finished and the General and his poor servant removed themselves back home.

Years later, after the General's death, his niece received a visit from a friend whose family now lived in Wrychtishousis. She compared notes with the servant, knowing he had once lived there, and sure enough they had the same story of the headless woman and her ghostly baby. When the building was being converted into a school and hospital years later, the built in cupboard in the room was removed to uncover boards which had clearly been removed at some stage and then re-laid. They lifted the boards to find a homemade coffin, containing the headless body of a woman and a small baby, inside a pillowcase, clutched to her chest. There was also a note from the murderer, explaining his guilt.

Apparently, many years before, the owner of the house had been sent to war and was killed, leaving his total inheritance to his infant son in the care of his young wife. The man's brother was outraged at this and in a fury, killed the mother and son so he could claim the inheritance for himself. In order to hide the evidence, he had made a coffin himself to bury them in, but his measurements were too short…so he cut off his sister in law's head to make her fit in the box!

In the area of the Botanic Gardens over a hundred years ago, a strange and solitary man lived at No.17 in a well-respected street. His only caller was a charwoman who would twice weekly come to his home to bring him his provisions. After his death, the charwoman locked the house tight and it lay empty for years, until stories began to circulate of late night parties on the upper floors, overheard by the residents of numbers 16 and 18. But no one was while, until it was mostly forgotten. Then, in the early throes of World War I, the house was completely gutted and converted into a guesthouse for an English couple, who then moved in to run the house.

The first signs that something was not right came when two different chambermaids claimed to hear voices from an attic bedroom, but upon entering, found the room empty. The room was generally not used, because of these unnatural occurrences, until the guesthouse came to be overbooked and a young married couple were given the keys for the attic room. On approaching the door, they heard voices and assumed they had been given the wrong room number, so rang the bell for service. An old woman by the name of Mary Brewster responded and entered the room to prove there was nobody in there at all. But as soon as she entered she let out a shattering scream, and it was the last sound she ever made. She was found rigidly clinging to the bedpost, staring straight at the ceiling in terror, and although she survived, she never spoke another word.

News of this reached some local students and one, Andrew Muir, determined to sit alone in the room one night, with two bells, one small and one large. The small bell was to signal anything unusual happening, while the large bell was to be a call for aid to the owner, who was sitting in the downstairs room. At 10:00 pm Muir entered the room. After only ten minutes, the small bell was rung vigorously, immediately followed by the panicked clanging of the larger bell. The owner flew up the stairs and flung open the door to find Muir literally frightened to death in his chair, staring up at the ceiling.

The owners decided to retire and the house was boarded up again for the rest of its days, before the entire street was eventually demolished, taking with it whatever evil had shown itself to Mary and Andrew.

MARY KING'S CLOSE

While these ghosts are all from places which are no longer available to be seen, there are tales of ghosts in places that are still very much accessible to this day, too – most of which are in parts of the old Underground Edinburgh that has often been forgotten by history, but has always remained below the surface of the Old Town. There are two areas in which people can gain access to this underground world. The first is Mary King's Close. Long ago discovered again, this close runs directly underneath the City Chambers building on the High Street.

In 1645 a terrible plague gripped Edinburgh. Out of 40,000 occupants, only 60 citizens were deemed fit to guard the city and bear arms. In dramatic attempts to curb the spread amongst the walled in city, many areas were simply sealed up and the dying left

inside to rot. This was the case with Mary King's Close, and after the inhabitants had all died off, the city moved in to dismember the bodies, which were all transported to and buried under what are now the Meadows, on the south side of town. Over forty years later, Edinburgh's overcrowding problem was at a peak and so the close was re-opened for occupation. Thomas Coltheart, a lawyer, and his wife were the first to move in, upon which their maid immediately left their service, fearing the legendary ghosts of the close.

One night, not long into their stay, the Colthearts came across these ghosts… and then some. Mrs Coltheart was surprised to see the sudden appearance of a disembodied head above her husband, which he somehow managed to miss. Her begging for him to leave with her went unanswered. Later that night, however, Coltheart was to see the head himself, as the couple sat in bed, which spurred him directly to prayer. This seemed only to draw more ghostly figures, with first a small child and then a disembodied arm, which was intent on shaking hands with the couple. Coltheart entreated the ghosts to tell him what they wanted done and he would make right their desires, but they seemed to want nothing other than to harass the poor couple. Further children, animals, including a cat and a dog, and other body parts joined the scene until eventually there was no floor to be seen for ghostly shapes. Then, suddenly, there was an awful and resonant moan, and the ghosts were gone.

Now, you would think that most people would take that as a sign that they were not welcome, but not Mr Coltheart. He was determined to stay on and stay he did, without further reported interference, until the day of his death. At which time it seems that, on the moment of his death, a friend living on the south side of the city was visited by a cloud, which took the form of Coltheart before dissipating. It seemed that the other spirits had truly accepted Coltheart after all.

Today, there are many reports of ghostly activity still going on. A young boy is rumoured to have died, trapped in one of the close's chimneys, and can be heard trying to scratch his way to freedom. The ghost of a small girl named Sarah has also been frequently seen haunting the kitchen of the old Royal Exchange Coffee Rooms, where it has become a tradition to leave a doll for her to make her happy. The main ghosts seem to be mostly at rest these days though, with the occasional exception, like the party of nurses who spent the night in the close for charity and complained of no ghosts, but that the party in the pub upstairs had kept them awake all night. Of course, they were directly below the City Chambers, which was locked up tight for the night and completely abandoned.

By far the most haunted place in Edinburgh's Underworld though, has turned out to be the Vaults underneath South Bridge. There are so many different tales of ghosts and hauntings in these vaults that they would probably sustain a book on their own. For example, there's the story of the two adventurous Canadian backpackers who found an uncovered old vent leading into one vault from Niddry Street. They decided to climb down and investigate, but once down there, both of their flashlights went out and they were lost in the dark for some hours, screaming for help and trying to find their way back to the vent. They eventually found it, only to discover it had been covered up from above. More screaming ensued until someone above heard them and removed the cover. They scrambled back up the shaft and onto the street, only to discover, to their horror, that despite neither of them feeling anything while they were down there, both of their faces were covered in bloody claw marks.

Two buildings on either side of the Bridge have been particularly famous for ghostly sightings. The first is the old Scotsman building, now the Scotsman Hotel, which is technically on the North Bridge, but not terribly far away. Years ago, an employee of the paper was down underneath the Bridge in one of the old vaults, which contained a lot of disused printing presses, when he came across a door he couldn't remember seeing before. Curious, he opened it and found a set of stairs stretching down below him. Halfway down, he saw one of his colleagues crossing the floor, but dressed in slightly outdated clothing. Suddenly, he had a terrifying realisation: the other printer was not making any sound. No footfalls, no breathing, not a single noise emanated from him. The employee raced back up the stairs to find his colleagues and tried in vain to explain what he'd seen. Dragging them back down to the vault for confirmation, they found only one door in the room, and it was soundly locked tight. Other encounters in the old building have included a security guard coming across an employee working late, literally, since he had died some time before and a regular visitor – a woman in black who frequented the reception area, irritating the staff.

The other building which has seen a fair amount of haunting is Whistle Binkie's, the pub that is set in the vaults just down on the east side of South Bridge. There were two ghosts that were known to frequent this pub: the Imp and the Watcher. The Imp was never actually seen, but had a terribly mischievous sense of humour. For example, one barmaid was frightened by him one night when collecting up glasses after closing time. She had taken out an orange to have as a snack and then spotted some glasses on a windowsill that she had missed. Leaving the orange on the counter, she crossed the bar to get them and turned to see her orange had been completely peeled and segmented for her.

Another barmaid, Kate Sinclair, found herself locked in the cellar of the bar, despite the door being unlocked. The Imp held the door shut against her, until she sat down and cried at her predicament, at which time the door swung open and allowed her to leave. He also took to regularly stopping the pub clock at 4:15 in the morning as well as moving things around and generally being a nuisance, but the Imp was never one for hurting anybody.

The Watcher was much the same, but had less direct interaction with people. But while nobody ever saw the Imp, many people saw the Watcher. He was described as tall, with long hair and wearing a long, heavy gentleman's coat of 17th Century style. One of the first to see him was a builder when Whistle Binkie's was first being built in the vaults not long ago. Coming into the pub, he saw what he thought was a woman in a heavy dress descending a set of stairs across the room. Chasing her, he found the stairs and the room below empty. The builder described the sight to a local historian, even drawing the figure's clothing, the historian pointed out that this was in fact a man's coat, not a dress. He had seen the Watcher. Both the Watcher and The Imp were known to also visit the rest of the South Bridge Vaults, with The Watcher even being mistaken for a tour guide by one group, who followed him into a room and then found it utterly empty. But neither of them made their home for long down there, because even they did not wish to stay around once the most frightening and malicious of Edinburgh's ghosts took up residence: the Mackenzie Poltergeist.

This presence has never been seen but manifests itself in many unpleasant and threatening ways. Since the occurrences attributed to it have come predominantly in two places, the vaults here and Greyfriars Kirkyard, it is believed to be the spirit of 'Bloody' Mackenzie, a vicious judge who worked for Charles I and ruthlessly pursued and murdered a religious group known as The Covenanters. Mackenzie's house was opposite the vaults in his lifetime, and his body now lies in the Kirkyard. He also had the personality to match the feeling that everyone who has encountered this spirit has attributed to it: pure evil.

The occurrences started in 1995, the year after the Vaults were first opened to tour parties. The first signs were the well-known phenomena of 'cold spots", where one place in a room would be ludicrously cold compared with the rest of it. Two Australian girls, Susan Harvey and Susan Douglas, were the first to encounter this when on a tour. They stood in a doorway to a vault and became suddenly cold. One of the girls felt nauseous and almost fell, but for her friend catching her. Then the other girl let out a terrible scream and backed into the vault, away from the door. As many others then checked and verified, despite the temperatures in the vault and the corridor being fine, the doorway's air was so cold as to be painful to the skin.

Many other were to experience similar occurrences in the coming months. Pole Maja Szeresewska, Canadian Jodi Stone and Americans Maggie Baker and Betsy Denton all had similar experiences, several of them fainting from the fright. Whatever was happening, it was only attacking women. In June 1996, the attacks got worse, as two different women, three days apart found themselves suddenly cold and then having an unseen hand forcing their heads down to the floor. In September of that year, a young boy was carried from the vaults unconscious and later explained that something freezing cold had been holding on to his head: so now it was also attacking children.

What did become clear though was that the attacks seemed to be centered around one vault, and one corner in particular: the left. This became known as 'The Haunted Vault'. This vault, it turned out, had quite a history of nasty occurrences, dating back to times when bands were briefly allowed to practice in them. Many electrical cables had to be run in, but the Haunted Vault was having none of it. No band ever wanted to work in there and eventually it became so damp, that the wiring had to be removed and the enterprise abandoned. Once the bands were gone, the moisture went too. This same phenomenon was also known to affect a White Witches Coven, who were given permission to use one of the vaults for a temple. They placed a mirror in the room, as was standard. Despite their room having been dry and warm on entering, it quickly became so wet as to be uninhabitable. More frighteningly, it appeared that the mirror became not just a mirror, but as one visiting psychic described it 'a door, letting in evil'. Many children complained of being frightened by 'The Man from the Mirror' in other parts of the vault and so the temple was eventually abandoned and the mirror disposed of.

Anyway, back to the Haunted Vault. It transpired on further investigation that even more disturbing events had taken place, with people sighting strange lights in the chambers, including several instances of a cross-shaped light that faded or changed shape as it was approached. One light seemed to be particularly attracted to a young Scottish girl, who came back again days later to see the light, and the light came back to see her. Many other such incidents occurred including attacks on children and the occasional man and even a small dog that was once allowed to accompany his master down but would absolutely not suffer to be taken into the Haunted Vault, howling and wailing as his master tried to take him in. Pets were thereafter banned from the tours.

One particularly chilling experience happened to Marion Duffy

to turn on their flashlights. Marion immediately heard Claire gasp and then grab her hand in the dark. Just as the story came to an end, Claire's grip tightened on Marion's hand, so much so as to be painful and Marion cried out. Then the lights came on and Marion looked down at her daughter…who wasn't there. She was standing a good 15 feet away. She then explained that when the lights went out she had reached for her mother's hand, and the hand she found had slowly led her through the dark to where she stood, before disappearing when the lights came on. Claire was standing exactly in the left hand corner of the vault.

Figuring out the pattern that Mackenzie was only attacking women on the left side of the vault, the tour guides started to organise them so that all the men were on the left and women on the right. The attacks stopped. On the tourists. And started on the guides – the female ones anyway, who were punched and knocked to the ground in the vault. They quickly went back to letting people stand wherever they liked.

These days the sightings are less frequent and tend to be spread between both the vaults and Greyfriars Kirkyard. Perhaps Old Mackenzie got bored of attacking women and children, or perhaps he's just having a rest, before coming back with a vengeance. Either way, you could count yourself unlucky to experience his icy touch these days. Less common as the attacks may be though, they still happen and the vaults still carry their eerie atmosphere.

A few years ago, a group of students were led into the vaults for an experiment, which was later televised. Each of them was asked to spend the night alone in the dark in one of the vaults, while night vision cameras watched them. They were not told which vault was which. If memory serves, the girl in the Haunted Vault spent most of her time agitated and scared and later claimed she was absolutely certain there had been someone else sitting in the dark with her. So if you're looking for an extra normal experience, the Haunted Vault is still probably the best place to start…

If you want to read more about Edinburgh's dark side, I recommend the following books, which were instrumental in putting this collection together, by filling in details of stories I'd heard and introducing me to some new ones too:

The Town Below the Ground, by Jan-Andrew Henderson and *Ghostly Tales & Sinister Stories of Old Edinburgh*, by Wilson, Brogan and McGrail. Both are published in Scotland by Mainstream Publishing and are available in major Edinburgh

find your way

If you need some assistance finding your way around Edinburgh, our handy maps should be able to help you. The main map here shows where our six main areas are in relation to the rest of the city, and each of the individual maps has our advertisers located on it and an index of the page numbers where you'll find information on that area throughout the book. Happy exploring.

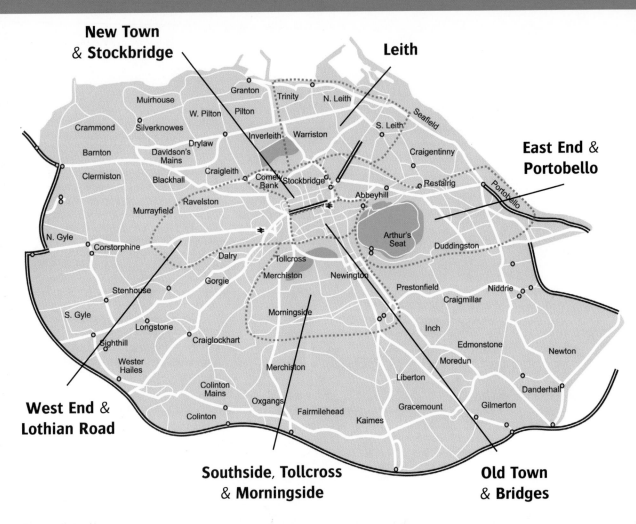

New Town & Stockbridge

Leith

East End & Portobello

West End & Lothian Road

Southside, Tollcross & Morningside

Old Town & Bridges

Granton
Trinity
N. Leith
Muirhouse
W. Pilton
Pilton
Seafield
Crammond
Silverknowes
S. Leith
Drylaw
Inverleith
Warriston
Craigentinny
Barnton
Davidson's Mains
Craigleith
Clermiston
Blackhall
Comely Bank
Stockbridge
Restalrig
Abbeyhill
Portobello
Ravelston
Murrayfield
Arthur's Seat
Duddingston
N. Gyle
Corstorphine
Dalry
Tollcross
Merchiston
Newington
Prestonfield
Niddrie
Gorgie
Craigmillar
Stenhouse
S. Gyle
Morningside
Inch
Longstone
Edmonstone
Newton
Sighthill
Craiglockhart
Moredun
Wester Hailes
Merchiston
Liberton
Danderhall
Colinton Mains
Oxgangs
Gracemount
Gilmerton
Colinton
Fairmilehead
Kaimes

New Town & Stockbridge

	PAGE
Sightseeing	15-16
Shopping	25-33
Eating out	41-46
Drinking	60-62
Entertainment	67-68

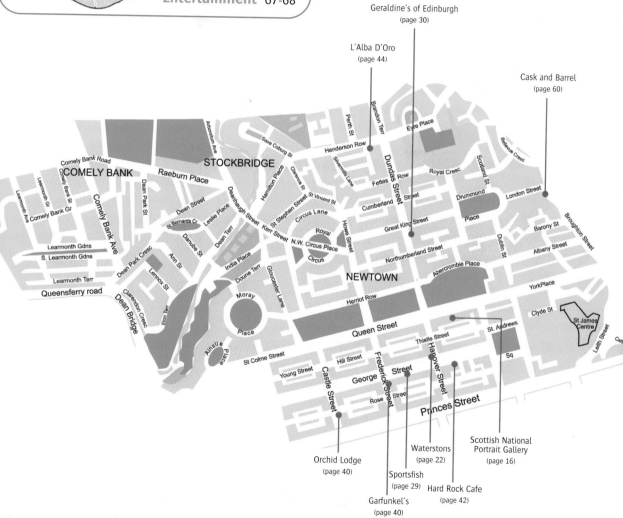

Geraldine's of Edinburgh
(page 30)

L'Alba D'Oro
(page 44)

Cask and Barrel
(page 60)

Orchid Lodge
(page 40)

Sportsfish
(page 29)

Garfunkel's
(page 40)

Waterstons
(page 22)

Hard Rock Cafe
(page 42)

Scottish National
Portrait Gallery
(page 16)

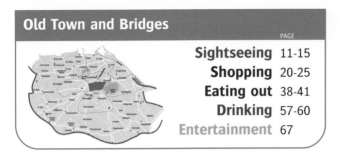

Old Town and Bridges

	PAGE
Sightseeing	11-15
Shopping	20-25
Eating out	38-41
Drinking	57-60
Entertainment	67

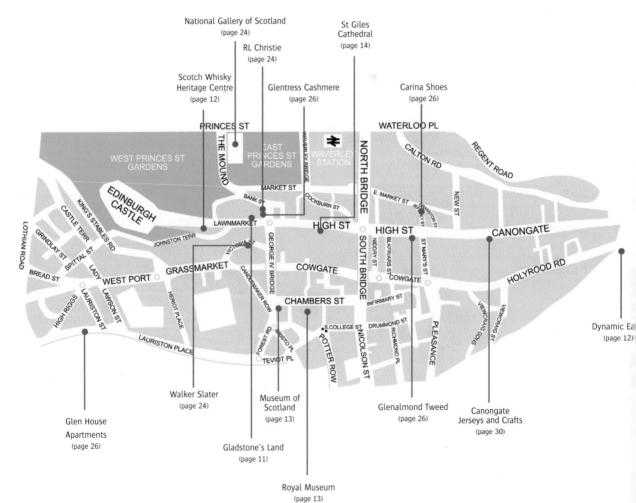

National Gallery of Scotland
(page 24)

RL Christie
(page 24)

St Giles
Cathedral
(page 14)

Scotch Whisky
Heritage Centre
(page 12)

Glentress Cashmere
(page 26)

Carina Shoes
(page 26)

Dynamic Ea
(page 12)

Walker Slater
(page 24)

Museum of
Scotland
(page 13)

Glenalmond Tweed
(page 26)

Canongate
Jerseys and Crafts
(page 30)

Glen House
Apartments
(page 26)

Gladstone's Land
(page 11)

Royal Museum
(page 13)

West End and Lothian Road

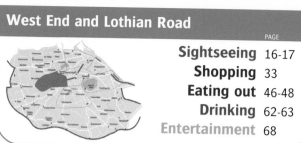

	PAGE
Sightseeing	16-17
Shopping	33
Eating out	46-48
Drinking	62-63
Entertainment	68

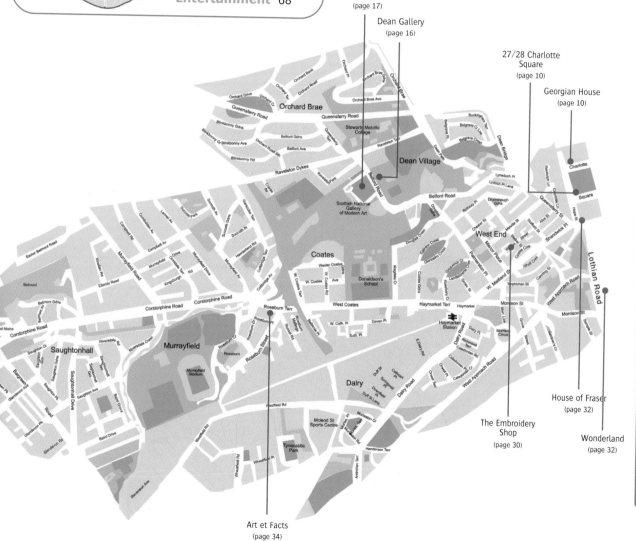

Scottsih National
Gallery of
Modern Art
(page 17)

Dean Gallery
(page 16)

27/28 Charlotte
Square
(page 10)

Georgian House
(page 10)

House of Fraser
(page 32)

Wonderland
(page 32)

The Embroidery
Shop
(page 30)

Art et Facts
(page 34)

Southside, Tollcross and Morningside

Tollcross

Lauriston Pl

Edinburgh
Royal
Infirmary

George
Square

South Bridge

St Leonards

The Meadows

The Meadows

Mellville Terr

Bruntsfield
Links

Polwarth

Bruntsfield

Warrender Park Terr

Warrender Pk Road

Royal
Hospital
For Sick
Children

Newington

Merchiston

Marchmont

Grange

Salisbury Rd

Churchill

Strathearn Road

Hope Terrace

Blackford Road

Grange Loan

George
Watsons
College

Newbattle Terr

Grange Loan

Royal
Blind
School

Astley
Ainslie
Hospital

West Savile Terrace

Camer
Toll

Royal
Edinburgh
Hospital

Morningside

Oswald Rd

S. Oswald Rd

Mortonhall Rd

Camero
Toll
Shoppin
Cente

Nile Grove

Cluny Ave

Charterhall Rd

Blackford Avenue

West Mains Road

Cluny Gardens

Cluny Gardens

East End and Portobello

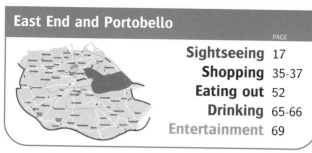

	PAGE
Sightseeing	17
Shopping	35-37
Eating out	52
Drinking	65-66
Entertainment	69

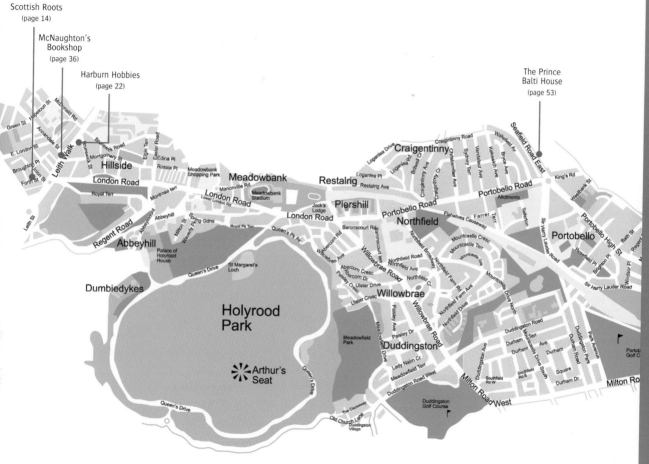

Scottish Roots
(page 14)

McNaughton's
Bookshop
(page 36)

Harburn Hobbies
(page 22)

The Prince
Balti House
(page 53)

Green St
E. London St
Broughton Pl
Forth St
Hughesoun St
McDonald Rd
Leith Walk
Union Pl
Annandale St
Leith St
Brunswick St
Montgomery St
Brunswick Road
Edina Pl
Elgin Terr
Exeter Road
Rosaie Pl

Hillside

London Road
Royal Terr
Montrose Terr
Regent Road
Abbeyhill
Milton St
Spring Gdns
Waverley Pk Terr
Royal Pk Terr
Abercorn
London Road
Lower London Rd
Marionville Rd
Meadowbank
Shopping Park

Meadowbank

Meadowbank
Stadium
Jock's
Lodge
London Road

Abbeyhill

Palace of
Holyrood
House
Queen's Drive
St Margaret's
Loch

Dumbiedykes

Queen's Pk Av
Queen's Drive

Holyrood
Park

☀ Arthur's
Seat

Queen's Drive
Queen's Drive
The Causeway
Old Church Lane
Duddingston
Village

Restalrig
Restalrig Ave
Loganlea Rd
Loganlea Pl

Craigentinny
Loganlea Drive
Loganlea
Bithell Cres
Craigentinny Ave
Craigentinny Cr
Craigentinny Rd
Christiemiller Ave
Craigentinny Road
Wakefield Av
Sydney Terr
Vandeleur Ave
Keddach Ave
Bryce Ave

Piershill
Baronscourt Rd
Baronscourt Terr

Northfield
Portobello Road
Portobello Road
Fishwives Causeway
Farrer Terr
Tarferton

Willowbrae Road
Abercorn Rd
Abercorn Cresc
Abercorn Dr
Ulster Drive
Ulster Cresc
Paisley Cresc

Mountcastle Cresc
Mountcastle Terr
Mountcastle Cres
Northfield Broadway
Northfield Farm Rd
Northfield Ave
Northfield C
Northfield Rd
Northfield Farm Ave
Northfield Drive

Willowbrae

Willowbrae Road

Meadowfield
Park
Paisley Av
Meadowfield
Drive

Duddingston
Lady Nairn Cr
Meadowfield Terr
Duddingston Road West

Duddingston
Golf Course

King's Rd
Westbank St
Seafield Road East
Sir Harry Lauder Road
Portobello High St
Bath St
Reginald
Rosefield Pl
Brighton Pl
Windsor Pl
Portobello Road
Allotments

Portobello

Sir Harry Lauder Road

Duddingston Road
Duddingston Ave
Durham Terr
Durham
Mountcastle Dr
Mountcastle Drive North
Mountcastle Drive South
Durham Ave
Durham Road
Durham
Square
Durham Dr
Southfield
Rd W
Southfield
Rd E

Milton Road West
Milton Rd
Park Avenue
Portobello
Golf C

Leith

	PAGE
Sightseeing	18
Shopping	37
Eating out	52-56
Drinking	66
Entertainment	69

Royal Yacht
Britannia
(page 18)

Waterfront Wine Bar
(page 54)

Ocean Blue
(page 56)

Daniel's Bistro
(page 56)

James Pringle Weavers
(page 36)